kamera
B O O K S

Pocket Essentials by this author

RIDLEY SCOTT
LAUREL AND HARDY
JAMES CAMERON

Brian J. Robb

SILENT CINEMA

kamera
BOOKS

First published in Great Britain in 2007 by Kamera Books
PO Box 394, Harpenden, Herts, AL5 1XJ

Copyright © Brian J. Robb 2007
Series Editor: Hannah Patterson

A CIP catalogue record for this book is available from the British Library.

ISBN-13: 978-1-904048-63-3

Book typeset by Elsa Mathern
Printed by SNP Lefung Printers (Shenzen) Co Ltd, China

CONTENTS

SILENT CINEMA: AN INTRODUCTION

From its beginnings as a series of Victorian novelties, the new art and industry of cinema rapidly developed in the first years of the twentieth century to become a distinct art form in its own right. Some would claim it was the definitive art form of the twentieth century. The 30-year period from the end of the nineteenth century through to the coming of sound in 1929 saw dramatic technological and aesthetic change in the cinematic arts. The result was the period of silent cinema when film had a distinctive form, and directors and actors worked within a set of growing and changing artistic criteria. It was unique and virtually ended when Al Jolson uttered the immortal words 'You ain't heard nothin' yet' in 1927's *The Jazz Singer.*

Technological experimentation to create moving images started as a quest by a series of individuals across Europe but rapidly became the concern of commercial organisations that saw the development of a new medium that could be exploited financially. From the earliest days cinema was torn between art and commerce. The first films (merely recordings of 'reality' projected back to an audience) were simple, but as creative techniques – such as editing, moveable cameras, studio and location shooting – emerged, cinema became more complex. By the time an audience had formed for film and the days of vaudeville were numbered, a creative critical mass had also collected around the production side of the cinematic equation.

The developing art of cinema saw a series of individuals working within commercial entertainment organisations drive the form forward

⌐h stylistic and technological innovation. No one individual invented 'cinema' as we know it, but skilful practioners such as Georges Méliès, DW Griffith, Cecil B. DeMille and Charlie Chaplin all pushed the boundaries of the medium.

The rise of film saw the creation of a star system as fictional narratives came to dominate the form. The likes of Mary Pickford, Douglas Fairbanks and Charlie Chaplin became the biggest stars of their age through audience adoration. Known around the world – as silent cinema knew no language barriers – these stars came to live extraordinary lives. Their unique status would lead to the US film colony of Hollywood becoming known as a city of sin where people lived by their own rules. A series of scandals in the 1920s – from the Roscoe 'Fatty' Arbuckle murder trial to the unexplained death of starlet Olive Thomas – would bring censure and censorship down upon the movies. It seemed that the new entertainment format of film also had a dark side.

The silent clowns – prime among them Chaplin, Buster Keaton and Harold Lloyd – showed that Hollywood also had a lighter side. However funny these guys – and others like Ben Turpin, Harry Langdon and Charley Chase – were, their lives were often fraught with difficulty and tragedy, from Chaplin's multiple relationships, to Lloyd's near fatal accident and Keaton's inability to handle his own finances. While they made audiences cry with laughter, these great screen clowns of the silent age were often the 'crying on the inside' type.

Silent cinema wasn't all Hollywood-based, of course. Serving as an informed introduction to the wider subject, this volume briefly acknowledges significant silent film production in Germany (the Expressionist classics *The Cabinet of Dr Caligari* and *Metropolis*), Italy (the epics *Quo Vadis?* and *Cabiria*), France (the Impressionist serial *Fantomas*, and Abel Gance's *Napoléon*) and Russia (home of political montage editing, as seen in the work of Eisenstein in *Battleship Potemkin*).

A quick survey of the 29 classics of silent cinema listed in detail in this book shows significant work from France, Germany, Sweden, Russia/

USSR and the UK, alongside that from the US, indicating the international reach of silent cinema.

That the first 30 years of cinema's history can be regarded as a unique and separate era of filmmaking is beyond dispute. This book celebrates the history and art of silent cinema, serving to introduce the curious film fan to the wonders of *Metropolis*, the lyricism of *Sunrise* and the artful comedy of Buster Keaton's classic *The General*. There is more silent era material available now than ever before through DVD, with many films restored and released in forms true to their creators' original intentions. Complete careers – such as those of Charlie Chaplin, Buster Keaton and Harold Lloyd – are widely available for us to view. There is extensive written material on all the topics explored in this introductory tome available in print or on the web. The resources section at the back of the current volume provides a jumping off point. That's what this book is intended to be: a place to begin your explorations of the era of silent cinema.

THE ORIGINS OF CINEMA

THE PRE-HISTORY OF CINEMA

Images were nothing new in the Western world of the industrial revolution period. The art of capturing images in paint (whether on cave walls or canvas) had existed from the earliest times, while still photography had been invented in 1827. Persistence of vision – the way the brain perceives rapidly changing still images as moving – was well known and formed the basis of many Victorian novelties.

From the creation of the 'magic lantern' in 1640, the goal of many visual artists had been to capture 'moving images'. The magic lantern could produce a series of single images projected in sequence upon a wall, illuminated by candlelight and later oil lamp, which told a story. From then to the invention of moving pictures, most devices that created the illusion of movement from still images were regarded as mere amusements or novelties.

A simple spinning disc held on a string with pictures on either side – called the Thaumatrope – would combine the two images, say a bird and a cage, into one: an image of a caged bird. Belgian Joseph Antoine Plateau invented the Phenakistoscope in 1832, producing a disc with a series of evenly spaced slits cut into it. On one side the disc featured drawings representing a simple movement, with a slight change in position between each image. Spinning the disc and viewing the images in a mirror through the slits in the spinning disc, the drawings would appear to move continuously.

Building upon Plateau's proof of persistence of vision, William George Horner came up with the Zoetrope. Drawing on the same principles, the Zoetrope consisted of a cylinder with evenly spaced slits cut into the top. Inside was placed a cartoon strip-like series of drawings, again attempting to capture a series of small movements. When the cylinder was spun and the images viewed through the slits (as with the Phenakistoscope), the illusion of movement was achieved. It wasn't until many years later, in 1867, that the Zoetrope was widely sold as an amusement. Similarly, the Phasmatrope, the 'projecting Phenakistoscope' and many other inventions kept the Victorians amused by creating the illusion of limited movement through drawings. There was little attempt to use these limited devices for any kind of narrative, or to develop them technologically.

It was the investigations into motion studies by photographer Eadweard J. Muybridge in 1877 that would lead directly to moving pictures. Muybridge was a British photographer who had made his name marketing photographic views of America in the 1860s. His initial creation of a series of photographs of a horse taken milliseconds apart was the result of a bet. Leland Stanford, the former Governor of California, hoped to prove that during a gallop all four hooves of a horse were off the ground simultaneously. Stanford hired Muybridge to prove his contention. The problem of achieving the technical requirements was only solved with the involvement of John D. Isaacs, chief engineer for the Southern Pacific Railroad. He knew nothing about photography but was able to apply his knowledge of mechanics, creating a system of magnetic releases to trigger the cameras photographing the horse in action. Muybridge shot a series of still photographs as a horse cantered past a row of twelve cameras. He then checked the images to see if any showed all four hooves off the ground. Stanford won his bet, though his expenditure to achieve his proof hugely exceeded the amount he eventually won.

Muybridge subsequently exhibited his series of horse photographs on tour, adapting them to various projection devices such as the Praxinoscope, the Zoetrope and others. He would go on to conduct other 'motion studies' with a variety of other subjects, including elephants,

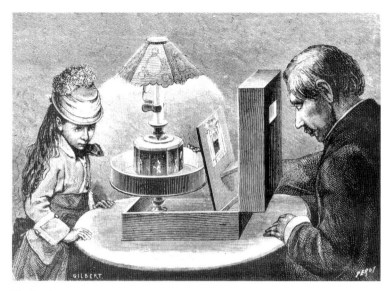

The Praxinoscope

domestic pets, farm animals and, eventually, people. An added frisson was brought to Muybridge's people studies as all his subjects were photographed nude. While he claimed educational purposes in touring his projections of these 'motion studies', no doubt Muybridge was a showman who knew the value of selling taboos to curious audiences. Muybridge even pioneered a form of stop motion animation as he took his human motion studies to their ultimate conclusion: a series of photographs of a skeleton moved into various poses to simulate life and then projected. Bizarrely, essentially the same multiple still camera set-up used by Muybridge in cinema's pre-history would be used to create the 'bullet time' effect in The Matrix (1999) and its sequels over 100 years later, well into the digital age of cinema.

Whatever his motivations, Eadweard Muybridge had shown one thing beyond any doubt: there was more to moving pictures than Victorian parlour games. In doing so, he'd also proved that there was a curious audience for such moving image diversions.

THE INVENTION OF CINEMA

If the invention of cinema was to be compared to one of the many genres which later came to dominate the art form, it might be regarded as a whodunnit. Given the claims and counterclaims for the sole right to be known as the inventor of cinema, perhaps the specific whodunit in question is JB Priestly's *An Inspector Calls*, in which everyone has some degree of culpability. Among the 'suspects' were American Thomas Alva Edison; the French Lumière brothers, Louis and Auguste; British-based Frenchman Augustin Louis Le Prince; and the British William Friese-Greene. Like movies themselves, however, the hunt for the sole inventor of cinema is an illusion.

The projection of moving images was a result of industrial development, rather than the inspired 'Eureka' moment of a lone inventor. From the beginning of the 1890s, conditions had developed which allowed for the progress of cinema technology primarily in four countries: the still-youthful Republic of America and the prime older nations of Europe – Britain, France and Germany. The end-of-the-century rush to cinema was driven by the profits to be made through commercial competition, rather than the romance of individual invention.

In 1884 George Eastman devised a way of manufacturing film on a roll (initially on paper, then celluloid) rather than in the form of individual slides, as had been the practice for still photography. By the end of the 1880s, Frenchman Louis Le Prince had patented a device for recording moving images on film and had used the large, cumbersome machinery he'd created to film trams and people from Leeds Bridge. This 1888 film – one of the earliest which still survives, shot on one of Eastman's paper film rolls – was only viewable with an Edison Kinetoscope, allowing the moving images to be seen by just one person at a time. Projection – which would allow a large number of people to simultaneously view moving images – was the goal, one that Le Prince never cracked. Eastman, however, returned to the fray, perforating his new celluloid film rolls with a series of holes, which allowed them to be driven through a camera and a projector. The only problem was that each individual frame had to momentarily stop in front of the lens to be exposed. It was the French Lumière brothers who solved this engineering challenge by adapting sewing machine technology. They created a camera smaller than that of Le Prince (who was to mysteriously vanish travelling on a train between Dijon and Paris in 1890, along with his briefcase of patent applications), dubbed the Cinématographe, which could also project the images it captured. Another innovation that contributed to the overall development of the early technology of cinema came from the entrepreneurial American Latham family who discovered a way of ensuring that the film running through the camera didn't suddenly break by running the reels loosely rather than tightly wound.

This was a nascent industry dominated by patents and piracy. Thomas Edison is prime among those whose names are associated with the invention of cinema, and his interest in moving pictures had begun seriously in 1887, two years after William Friese-Green's limited moving image experiments in Britain. Muybridge had met Edison in 1888 and they discussed Edison's invention of the light bulb and the phonograph. The result of those inventions was his company Edison General Electric, which was able to fund a whole programme of research. The truth of the discovery/invention process is that Edison himself did very little work on any apparatus. It was his team of employees who developed the first film cameras and projection equipment in America. Where his own team could not solve a problem, or someone else got there first, Edison's company would rapidly buy up the rights. For Edison, like so many after him, the success of cinema would be in its commercial exploitation not in the equipment that merely solved the problem of creating moving pictures.

It was an Edison employee, William KL Dickson, who is credited with the discovery – in 1891 – of a way to record images on a strip of celluloid which, when projected back, gave the illusion of movement. The machine – dubbed the Kinetograph – was used to create an early film, *Fred Ott's Sneeze* (1891), featuring one of Edison's workers... well, sneezing.

Edison applied for patents on the earliest film equipment, starting in 1893, and so it was his name that became attached to the creation of the film camera, projection equipment and the invention of motion picture film, even though others had made the discoveries or contributed in a major way. Despite his attention to commercial detail, Edison failed to expand his patents to Europe, so allowing the pioneers in moving image technology there to make their own claims to primacy of discovery.

Edison was to begin the commercial exploitation of cinema in 1896 and by the following year he was merrily suing others to protect the integrity of his patents for the movie camera. This model of the creation and exploitation of new technology was the common experience in the nineteenth century, so no one saw any particular problem with it or with Edison's activities.

In the early years, cinema was seen as an industrial process rather than a creative art. Money was to be made in the building, selling and licensing of the equipment to make and project films. The creation of the films themselves was almost regarded as a side-effect: in today's parlance, they were the software needed to drive the hardware sales, athough the industrial model was the inverse of that for modern computing where the money was to be made in the hardware (the cameras and projectors) rather than the software (the films).

The immediate precursor of properly projected cinema – and thus the group experience that was so important to the impact of the art form – was the individually viewed, Edison-invented Kinetoscope device. The Kinetoscope – supplied to amusement arcades across the world – helped to create the idea that the money to be made in cinema was in the hardware. Viewed by one person at a time using the 'What the Butler Saw' machines, the Kinetoscope created in the public the idea of proper moving images, paving the way for projected cinema.

By February 1893, the year of the Chicago World's Fair where the Kinetoscope made its public debut, Edison had established the world's first dedicated film studio to create films for his Kinetoscope machines. Dubbed the 'Black Maria', the studio lacked a roof as it used sunlight for illumination. The entire thing had been built upon a pivot so it could be rotated to take best advantage of the position of the sun. It was in the Black Maria that Edison's assistant Dickson embarked upon the creation of a series of films recording the acts of leading vaudeville performers, including 'Buffalo Bill' Cody and Annie Oakley. *Fun in a Chinese Laundry* (1894) was a film record of a well-known vaudeville sketch, while *Execution of Mary Queen of Scots* (1895), made by Alfred Clark after Dickson's departure, is a historical reconstruction. These Kinetoscope films lasted less than a minute each.

It is the French Lumière brothers, however – Auguste and Louis – who are usually credited with being the first to publicly screen movies before an audience on a large screen, in Paris on 28 December 1895, widely recognised as the official birth date of cinema. At the time the Lumière brothers were the biggest manufacturer of photographic plates in Europe. Their dramatic programme of films was also screened to a paying audience in Britain on 20 February 1896 at the Regent Street Polytechnic, hosted by a representative of the Lumières. Edison himself followed with a demonstration of his equipment on 23 April 1896 at Koster and Bial's Music Hall in New York City. Within months, exhibitors in France, the United Kingdom and the United States could screen films to large paying crowds at once using just one projecting machine.

Screened at the Grand Café at 14 boulevard des Capucines, and promoted by an enthusiastic street barker, the December 1895 Lumière programme included the now famous early film *L'Arrivée d'un train en gare de La Ciotat* (*The Arrival of a Train at La Ciotat Station*, 1895), along with other 'actuality' films which chronicled workers leaving the Lumière factory, footage of Auguste Lumière and family eating breakfast, and members of the Congress of Photographic Societies milling around (which had been shot and screened for the membership on the same day). This first historic film screening took place in the basement of the café, known as the Salon Indien, where 35 spectators were to witness what's now regarded as the official debut of moving pictures. Among those present were the director of the Folies-Bergère and the head of the popular Grévin wax museum, as well as Georges Méliès, magician and director of the Théâtre Robert-Houdin.

Lumières Cinematographie

Filmed from a low-angle, almost level with the railway track itself, the action of *L'Arrivée d'un train en gare de La Ciotat* consisted of a single shot of a train pulling into the station, gradually getting larger in the frame as it approached the fixed camera position. Legend has it that audiences, fearing that the image of the train might crash through the screen itself, dived under their seats, screamed and fainted or rushed for the exits. The impact was compared to that of being on a rollercoaster, itself invented in 1884 – the same year as Eastman's film rolls.

The Lumières got into filmmaking as local Kinetoscope proprietors were looking for a source of films for their machines, cheaper than those from the Edison company. Within weeks, the Lumières were offering 20 shows a day, with long lines of would-be spectators forming around the block, around the clock. Keen to cash in on their new sensation, the Lumières rapidly despatched copies of their various films, the projection equipment and the men to operate it, around the globe. Audiences from Italy to Canada, India to Mexico and Argentina marvelled at the stately arrival of that French train.

In America, Edison had screened his films using a machine dubbed Edison's Vitascope (a projection machine Edison had actually bought from its inventors, C. Francis Jenkins and Thomas Armat). Six films were included in the programme, most originally made for Edison's Kinetoscope. Singled out for particular praise was a non-Kinetoscope film, *Rough Seas at Dover* (1895), a dramatic single shot of waves crashing against a sea wall. This demonstration rapidly prompted the Keith Theatre Circuit, a vaudeville (variety entertainment) chain, to invest in the new sensation of cinema. Interestingly, the Keith Circuit bought a licence for the French Lumière brothers' equipment rather than Edison's. The distinguishing factor was that the French equipment could run from stand-alone generators, whereas Edison's had to be plugged into the local power supply (which were, at the time, non-standard across America and controlled by local municipal power companies). This was the beginning of the battle over standards for early cinema, which saw different film formats fitting different company's equipment, and exhibitors tied to individual manufacturing and film production companies.

Dickson, Edison's erstwhile assistant, had gone into business with Herman Casler, forming the American Mutoscope Company in 1896 to exploit Dickson's development work on cameras and projectors, which had previously benefited Edison. The Mutoscope – a development of the Kinetoscope – used 70mm film, rather than Edison's standard 35mm films, and produced larger and clearer images, resulting in American Mutoscope becoming the most popular film company in America by 1897, dominating the peepshow machine market.

The first films were intended to be screened as an additional attraction alongside the live entertainment of vaudeville, rather than as an attraction in their own right. The backing of such a well-regarded promoter for the new technology as the Keith Circuit caused competing theatre chains to pay attention to the newly forming business of cinema. Others began to include novelty films as part of their vaudeville line-ups and the films rapidly came to eclipse the live performers in terms of popularity, attracting audiences across America of one million or more every week.

TECHNOLOGICAL INNOVATION

The earliest years of cinema saw the development of technological innovations that would not become commonplace for 60 years or more in some cases. For example, widescreen cinema is widely connected to the late-1950s and early-1960s, when cinema was battling against television for audience attention. However, American Enoch J. Rector had used widescreen film (63mm instead of the standard 35mm) to record an event billed as 'The Great Corbett Fight', a now long forgotten boxing match which took place in Nevada, but was viewed by audiences in Los Angeles and elsewhere across America. Rector invented a new camera to capture his widescreen images, which he dubbed the Veriscope. His film *The Corbett-Fitzsimmons Fight* (1897) captured the full width of the boxing ring within the film frame. With the art of editing in its infancy, this film is more-or-less a simple point-and-shoot record of the event, but one in which the spectacle was the attraction.

At the Paris Exhibition of 1900, at which cinema played a central role, the Lumière brothers played colour movies on a giant public screen, an innovation which would not become commonplace for another 50 years.

They also screened widescreen images, shot on 75mm film stock, larger than that eventually used for the 70mm widescreen epics of the late-1950s. Their innovations even extended to the screening of films with sound, provided through the replay of synchronised recordings. Filmgoers of today may think of the giant screens of Cinerama in the 1960s and 1970s, and the innovation of IMAX cinema in the 1980s, to be uniquely modern. Again, the Lumière brothers got there first with their display of 'Cinéorama' at the 1900 Paris Exhibition. The probably trepidatious audience sat on top of a circular projection box, which threw images onto a 330-foot, 360-degree screen, which featured ten separate but overlapping images. Innovative as it was, Cinéorama was only put into action twice as the ten projectors located under the audience created too much heat for the comfort of the viewers seated immediately above.

There were more successful cinematic innovations, though, some of which anticipated the theme park rides (many influenced by movies) that proliferated in the mid-late twentieth century. Taking movies beyond the mere illusion of movement and toward providing a more visceral sensation, Hale's Tours debuted at the 1903 St Louis Exposition. Named after its inventor George Hale, this attraction consisted of a converted railway carriage that audiences would board to enjoy the projection of moving images that simulated a train ride. In addition to the pictures projected onto a screen at the end of the carriage, the stationary train carriage would be rocked to replicate movement, while a narration and frequently interrupting train whistle and bell would provide an additional soundtrack, increasing the verisimilitude of the experience. Hale's Tours was eventually to become a travelling attraction seen across the United States.

These kinds of dramatic innovations this early in the development of cinema, however, indicate that the showmen of the late nineteenth century and the early twentieth century were not willing to be held back by technological limitations. If they could imagine it, they could invent a piece of equipment to achieve it. That colour, sound and giant screen films all had to wait until the previous industrial model of cinema had matured, and so was forced to change, is more a result of the commercial strictures of industrial development. Cinema now faces a similar turning point in the early twenty-first century with digital technology.

PUBLIC ACCEPTANCE OF CINEMA

By the end of the nineteenth century, cinema had become accepted as a form of entertainment alongside theatre and vaudeville. Often cinemas would be simple shop fronts like any other, sandwiched between stores serving people's daily needs. While filmmakers were developing their art, the public were consuming spectacle.

The spectacle of early cinema required large screen projection and large communal audiences for it to work. The individual consumption of moving images in forms such as Edison's Kinetoscope had long gone. Movies were now a communal, shared experience, to be enjoyed as part of a crowd, which could be wowed and moved as a single entity. In that respect, as in so many others, moving pictures were certainly emblematic of the twentieth century. With entrance fees in the United States ranging between five and ten cents, the movies were rapidly established as the cheapest form of mass entertainment available.

THE DEVELOPING ART

The history of the development of early cinema is one of accident, imagination, risk-taking and innovation, but most of all, trial-and-error. There were no rules for how this new medium could be used. The art of silent cinema would develop across many years and involve the aesthetic innovations of many individuals, groups and companies.

The dawn of the twentieth century – the century in which film would be the dominant art form – saw the consolidation of the cumulative lessons of four or five years of slow cinematic evolution. The potential of cinema had been recognised. Now it was down to those intrigued by the new medium, either for its own artistic possibilities or its commercial potential, to push film forward and to codify exactly what constituted the new art of 'cinema'.

DEVELOPING FILM GRAMMAR

Although many of the stylistic innovations that came to form the grammar of cinema were instigated or developed in Europe, the exploitation of the new medium rapidly moved west to the United States. As with so much industrial and scientific innovation in the nineteenth century, it was the 'new world' across the Atlantic that was best positioned to exploit the art and industry of filmmaking.

Following their 1895 claim to the first public film screening, the Lumière brothers were the first Europeans to establish the creation and distribution of moving pictures as a commercial business. Their success spurred on others, such as Brit Acres and RW Paul in the United Kingdom, who followed the Lumière's own Regent Street film demonstrations with their own regular screenings at the Alhambra music hall. In June 1896, Paul screened a film recording of that day's Derby race, which was viewed by – among others – the Prince of Wales, who owned the winning horse.

Paul would go on to make 50 or so films each year and came to dominate the British film business. In 1899, he built one of the first British film studios in Muswell Hill in London. Other significant figures on the early British filmmaking scene were Brighton portrait photographers GA Smith and Esme Collings, Cecil Hepworth – whose father had used magic lanterns to deliver lectures – and a fairground showman, Walter Haggar, from South Wales. Each of these entrepreneurs – and others – would develop the language of film through trial-and-error.

Their dramatic innovations were as much technical as artistic, each feeding the other: new equipment or new ways of using old equipment led to new on-screen artistic innovations. A prime case would be the invention of the camera 'dolly', a wheeled platform upon which a camera could be mounted and smoothly moved around. Invented in England in 1899 by RW Paul, the camera dolly gave filmmakers a new freedom in moving the camera, creating an intimacy between the audience and the events on screen. Liberating the camera from its previous static, fixed position was a simple innovation, but one which cannot be underestimated in its importance to on screen aesthetics.

In form, early cinema was heavily influenced by vaudeville, where the earliest films were screened alongside live performances. The likes of 'living pictures', phantasmagoric illusions and magic lantern shows – the visual novelties that preceded cinema – all provided generic and narrative shapes for the novelties of the earliest films.

Initially, movies were simply as long as the piece of celluloid that would fit in the equipment, mostly around 50 feet in length. It took ten to twelve of these short items to make up a complete vaudeville programme of fifteen minutes duration. The shortness of each item and the sheer novelty factor of projected images was enough to make cinema the latest modern marvel of the industrial age.

This public attitude to the first films may explain the producers lack of attention to quality: the fact that these pictures moved was often enough of a novelty to attract a large audience. The majority of early films were 'actualities', mere recordings of actual events featuring some conspicuously significant elements of movement. The famous example is the train arriving at a station, which in a typical vaudeville film show line-up may have been followed by people entering or leaving a factory (one part of the industrial revolution recording another, and often shot locally so offering audience members the added novel possibility of seeing themselves, relatives or friends moving on screen), shots of a beach or waves coming ashore, bicycles and other vehicles or animals. Audience tastes soon moved on from the mere marvel of pictures and moved to a demand for the exotic: they wanted to see moving pictures of things they couldn't see in everyday life. Thus was born the exotic subject: simple shots of far away places, dramatised incidents, re-enactments of famous events and recordings of exotic live entertainments, like the circus, acrobats or dancers.

Variety acts would be filmed and then projected, sometimes in the same vaudeville theatres, fictional narratives began to be developed, scenic views provided those who couldn't travel with moving postcards, topical events would be covered by film cameras spurring the beginnings of newsreels, and trick films began to develop as some filmmakers began to look at what could be done by manipulating the medium itself. Footage of disasters – or rather, their aftermath – became incredibly popular. The need for sensation in entertainment was born and continues to this day...

It didn't take long for those making the films to tire of filming the obvious and dishing it up to audiences. There were those who immediately saw the creative possibilities of the new medium and began to use film to do things that were unique to the form itself, armed with the new tools of editing and the close-up.

One of the significant British film pioneers was Brighton-based, still portrait photographer George Albert Smith, who'd rapidly taken to the new medium. Not content with the equipment created and leased by others, he built his own movie camera and set about making films. For *The Corsican Brothers* (1898), Smith developed the technique of multiple exposures. He shot a scene against a black velvet backdrop, in front of which his actors performed. He stopped the camera, wound back the film and then re-exposed the same piece of film on the same set, but replaced the previous actors with another playing a ghost, who on film appeared to float across the original scene.

This was not Smith's only innovation. Not content with simply shooting material and projecting it, he wondered what film would look like if it was projected in reverse. He also created a 'phantom ride' in which he attached a film camera to the front of a moving train and then projected the resulting film, giving audiences the illusion of uncontrollable speed: a dramatic step up from the graceful arrival of that train at La Ciotat.

The initial component of film as projected artifact was – and remains – the shot. The first films were simple, single shots, a record of an actual event happening in real time in front of the camera, uncut and unedited. Those making these films soon realised that it was possible to combine a series of shots to create a narrative, either of a real event or in retelling a fictional story. The introduction of editing, or 'cuts', sped up filmic storytelling. French director Georges Méliès (see the next chapter) was one of the first to implement simple associative editing in which one shot replaces another and the audience relates both images to make sense of what they're being shown. By 1898, multi-shot movies and films that had been carefully edited together were becoming commonplace. The 'rules' of editing were not yet set in place: more experimentation and the dawn of a new century would be required before internal film grammar would really blossom.

The new century brought other innovations. Smith continued to introduce new ways of playing with the images he was capturing on film. His *The Kiss in the Tunnel* (1899) featured cuts between a studio-filmed interior of a railway carriage and exterior shots filmed from the front of the train as it enters and leaves a tunnel. From such simple devices were the techniques of filmic narrative built. An early editing misfire featured characters looking off-screen (supposedly to indicate interior thought or memory) followed by shots that supposedly constituted those thoughts or memories. It soon became clear that audiences didn't understand these sequences and that technique rapidly fell by the wayside as others emerged which more economically established the same intention. For example, Smith's *Let Me Dream Again* (1900) featured one of the earliest examples of a 'focus pull', where the image goes from sharp to soft focus. Used as a less harsh transition between scenes than a straight cut, the focus pull created a closer connection between the two scenes it linked. In *Let Me Dream Again*, Smith softens the focus on a shot of a man kissing a beautiful woman, cuts the scene almost imperceptibly and then sharpens it again to show the man kissing his less than beautiful wife. This technique rapidly became associated with 'dream states' or fantasy images, capturing the thoughts and feelings of characters on-screen in a distinctly visual way.

In *Grandma's Reading Glasses* (1900), another film also by Smith, the director uses close-ups in a fashion not seen before. A sales catalogue entry promised the sight of objects 'in enormously enlarged form'. At this stage in the developing art of cinema, close-ups were explained through some form of technological intervention: images seen through keyholes, telescopes, or – in this case – eyeglasses. The dramatic use of the stand-alone close-up, laden with its own significant, context-dependent and unique meaning, was yet to come. Again, this development came in a George Albert Smith work called *The Little Doctor* (1901), a lost film, as so much of early cinema is. Not one to waste a good idea, Smith remade his own film two years later as *The Sick Kitten* (1903), in which a mastershot shows two children tending to a sick cat, followed by a cut to a close-up of the kitten as the children feed it medicine. There is no mediation of this close-up through a visual instrument or restricted viewpoint, no telescope or keyhole here. It's a simple progression, with Smith attempting to communicate his story – basic though it is – to his audience in a clearer manner, and in the process inventing one of the central building blocks of film grammar that still dominates commercial narrative cinema to this day. Smith realised that film was not theatre: viewpoint could be varied, rather than being restricted to the proscenium arch of classical theatre. The result was a freeing of cinema to tell stories in a different manner, one unique to the medium.

These innovations came slowly over a number of years as the fledgling art developed. James Williamson's *Fire!* (1902) established the use of visual continuity between shots to tell a story, while Cecil Hepworth's *Rescued by Rover* (1905) developed ideas of narrative storytelling further following the adventures of the title character, using careful framing and deploying a panning shot as the camera followed the movements of Rover the dog. By 1906, the fundamental features of narrative cinema had been developed, incorporating edited shots, insert shots (for example, a shot of what an on-screen character is looking at), dissolves and cross-fades between scenes or portions of scenes, moving cameras and panning shots, interspersed long-shots and dramatic close-ups.

THE MOVE WEST: PATENTS AND PROTECTION

As the new decade developed, the focus for film production and exhibition moved west, from Europe and the United Kingdom to New York and then, as a result of legal battles and attempts at monopoly largely by Edison, further west to California. It was in the United States that the art form of cinema would be developed into a successful world-dominating business. The consolidation of film grammar into the dominant American form was largely down to the work of two men in this period: Edwin S. Porter and David Wark Griffith.

Edison's battles to control the American film industry – and to restrict the potential success of incomers like the Lumière brothers and other French companies such as Pathé and Gaumont – had been a parallel to the development of on-screen syntax and storytelling. Competition between rival film producers and exhibitors was intense in the early days of the twentieth century. The 'nickelodeons', early cinemas where films could be individually viewed for a nickel – five cents – proliferated across the United States from 1905. Five years later, there were around 10,000 nickelodeons serving an estimated audience of 26 million people, around 20 per cent of the population, each week. This was growing into a big business, one which Edison had lost control of. His rivals, who now included Vitagraph, Mutoscope and Biograph, escaped being charged with patent infringement by building their own incompatible equipment. Edison even tried to claim a patent on the actual sprocket holes in the film everyone used, then locked Eastman into a contract to exclusively supply Edison with film, so determined was he to control the booming business of moving pictures.

As a bulwark against the arrival of foreign interests and to exert further control over those companies he couldn't intimidate or legislate out of business, Edison proposed the formation of the Motion Picture Patents Company in 1908, bringing his major former rivals under his paternalistic wing. Known as the Trust, this organisation controlled the majority of production and, through the General Film Company, distribution of US-manufactured films. Independent companies did not disappear altogether, despite the disruptive tactics of the Trust (which in some cases even extended to wild West-style gunfights in cinemas to enforce their monopolies).

It was within this context that Edwin S. Porter and David Wark Griffith both worked, developing their art (see Chapter 5: The Directors). Porter worked for the Edison company and Griffith for Biograph. These large companies provided a stable environment for both men to explore the craft of filmmaking. As the industry stabilised, films began to be created by specialist directors rather than the cameramen largely used in the early Lumière brothers films. As fictional narrative storytelling on-screen developed, directors and scenario writers (early scriptwriters) found roles in the film business. These directors often came from the theatre, where they had worked with actors who could now be persuaded to appear in these new-fangled 'moving pictures'. An unintended consequence of the use of stage talent combined with the developing use of the close-up, often featuring a focus on the human face, was the creation of the 'movie star' (see Chapter 6: The Dramatic Stars). The next four chapters will explore the roles of directors and movie stars – dramatic and comedic – in the continued development of the art of the silent cinema.

GEORGES MÉLIÈS:
INNOVATOR AND ENTERTAINER

The work of Georges Méliès is significant in realising the potential of early cinema. While credit for specific stylistic innovations often goes to American directors Edwin S. Porter or David Wark Griffith, Méliès often got there first. The fact that his use of techniques such as editing was often to conceal a cinematic trick rather in the furtherance of narrative (as with the work of Porter and Griffith) should not diminish Méliès' own significant achievements.

Born Marie Georges Jean Méliès in Paris on 8 December 1861. The youngest of three children, Méliès would follow a magical route to cinema. His Dutch mother and French father ran a successful footwear manufacturer. The young Méliès benefited from his mother's determination that her younger son should secure the formal education denied his older brothers, but which was now affordable to the family. His interests in drawing and puppetry were interrupted by his military service in 1881-1882 (a three-year commitment cut to one by his parent's 'donation' of 1,500 francs to the French armed forces). Hoping to train as a painter, Méliès found himself repaying this debt to his father by enrolling in the family business of boot manufacture.

Private art lessons (provided by the painter Gustave Moreau) were enough to satisfy Méliès' artistic ambitions while he learned his father's trade. Little did the young Méliès know he was learning technical and business skills that would stand him in good stead in his future show business endeavours. Spending a year in London in 1884 – both to formerly learn English and open up a branch of the family's shoe business – was a formative experience for Méliès. He found an outlet for his creative ambitions in London's theatrical milieu, where his limited command of English meant he had to focus on the purely visual, such as magic tricks and pantomime spectacles. Méliès quickly came to learn the tricks of the theatrical trade, discovering the behind-the-scenes secrets of theatrical illusion.

Méliès became an adept of renowned English magician John Nevil Maskelyne, partner in Maskelyne and Cooke's Egyptian Hall, London's specialist conjuring theatre. Maskelyne's big innovation was to combine narrative – storytelling – with his magic tricks, thus amusing and amazing his audiences. Méliès learned all he could from Maskelyne and from David Devant, another acclaimed London conjurer whose signature trick was to make a life-size portrait of a woman come to life on stage (featured in Méliès 1903 film *Le Portrait spirituel/The Spiritualist Photographer*, one of many Méliès films which drew on the tricks he learned in London, adapted to work more effectively on film).

Back in Paris in 1885, Méliès equally pursued his newfound interest in the magical arts and Eugénie Genin, daughter of a family friend, with equal vigour. Conveniently, his marriage provided the couple with a large dowry, meaning that Méliès did not have to return to the family trade and could pursue his growing theatrical ambitions: from shoe business to show business. In 1888, his father Louis retired and divided the business between his three sons. Méliès quickly sold his share to his brothers, raising enough money to enable him to fulfil a long-held dream of purchasing the Théâtre Robert-Houdin (co-incidentally located immediately below the photographic studio of Antoine Lumière, father of Auguste and Louis, on the Boulevard des Italiens). Founded by the renowned Jean-Eugène Robert-Houdin (from whom Houdini would take his stage name), who'd died in 1871, the theatre came especially equipped with trap doors, pulleys and other gimmicks to stage impressive magical entertainments. In his own newly refurbished venue, Méliès was able to further develop his

Georges Méliès in *Le Portrait spirituel*

art as a stage magician. Within a few years, Méliès was renowned for his innovative stage presentations that often involved the use of dramatic visual devices such as shadow puppets and magic lanterns. He spent numerous years working at the theatre developing new illusions, many of which featured actress Jehanne d'Alcy (who would go on to feature in many Méliès movies and become his second wife in 1925). Plenty of the illusions he developed here would later play a significant part in his films.

Méliès was one of those in attendance at the first Paris screening of a programme of film attractions by the Lumière brothers just after Christmas 1895 in the Salon des Indiens in the basement of the Grand Café. He was 34 years old and proclaimed himself to be 'filled with amazement'.[1] Struck by the potential of the new medium, Méliès rapidly established himself as one of the most important cinematic pioneers, whose work still has relevance for filmmakers facing the new challenges of the digital age.

Méliès began his cinematic explorations by contacting the Lumière brothers (they were local boys, after all) and asking to purchase one of their Cinématographes, combined cameras and projectors. Attempting to protect their newfound monopoly (just as Edison was doing in the United States), the Lumières refused Méliès' offer of the significant sum of 10,000 francs. Instead, Méliès was forced to turn to the United Kingdom and contacted RW Paul who had developed his own camera and projector and from whom Méliès was able to purchase a device for only 1,000 francs. By April 1896, Méliès was including films, purchased from Paul and Edison, in his theatrical shows, using Paul's equipment. Captivated by the new medium, it wasn't long before the inventive Méliès began to have thoughts about making his own films instead of just presenting other people's. To do so, he constructed his own camera and projection equipment.

In May (or June, historical accounts differ) 1896, Méliès shot his first movie in his own domestic garden in Montreuil, a suburb of Paris. The film – 17 metres long and lasting less than a minute – featured Méliès and his brother Gaston, as well as some friends, playing cards. It was imaginatively entitled *Une partie de cartes/Playing Cards* (1896).

Like most movie pioneers, Méliès' first films were simple 'actualities', straightforward filmed records of real events or simple street scenes, just like the work of the Lumière brothers, from which he initially took inspiration. Legend has it that Méliès' initial discovery of what more could be achieved with film was an accident: his camera momentarily jammed while filming in Paris. Viewing the result he discovered that the moment when the film jammed created a discontinuity in the on-screen action and the streetcars appeared to leap forward in space, while people walking past simply disappeared. This was a revelation to Méliès. The result was a willingness to experiment, leading to some of the earliest trick films, special effects driven movies, which pushed the nascent medium to the edge of its capabilities.

There is a dramatic division between the uses to which the Lumière brothers and Georges Méliès would put the new medium. Whereas

Voyage dans la lune/A Trip to the Moon (1902)

Auguste and Louis had come to film through the documentary medium of photography, Méliès came to cinema from the world of magical illusions. The Lumières saw film as a way to reproduce reality: a train arriving at a station, workers leaving a factory. Méliès saw film as a means to alter reality, to achieve on screen what was impossible in real life. He was not interested in merely photographing the real, but in capturing the unreal, the dream-like. Méliès had the advantage of his theatrical work, combining spectacle and narrative sympathetically. He could see the possibilities in 'using cinema not for the servile reproduction of nature, but for the spectacular expression of artistic and creative ideas of all kinds', as he wrote in his memoirs of 1912.[2]

One of Méliès' best-known films is *Voyage dans la lune/A Trip to the Moon* (1902), a particularly elaborate example of his early films. Often the titles of Méliès' movies would feature the words 'dream' or 'nightmare', clearly indicating that he was out to capture the unseen and unknowable on celluloid. During his first year in production, Méliès made 78 short films, many of them simple non-trick films, as he learned his way around the new medium. He soon progressed beyond what the Lumière brothers were achieving, however, with his first 'trick' film *The Vanishing Lady* (1896). In the film, Méliès appears as a magician whose trick involves transforming a woman into a skeleton. Based on his earlier stage exploits with Maskelyne, the simple cinematic trick was achieved by stopping the camera and replacing the woman in the scene with the skeleton. When projected, the jump cut made it appear as though one had instantly turned into the other. Later, Méliès would use stop-motion and other cinematic techniques to achieve more complex fantastic scenes. Until the mid-1920s, all his visual tricks were accomplished in the camera, with no laboratory post-production work possible at that time.

By 1897, Méliès had converted his theatre into a cinema and was now only screening films. He set up the world's first permanent film studio – beating Edison, who had the same idea to provide material for his Kinetoscopes – at Montreuil, where he embarked upon a unique process of cinematic creation. Like Edison's open-ceiling studio in New York, Méliès' was made of glass (resembling a large greenhouse) to allow natural light to illuminate his film productions. Méliès designed, built and painted elaborate backdrops for his films, painted on canvas flats and mimicking stage sets created for the theatre.

Just before the turn of the century, Méliès seemed to be concentrating on developing his cinematic techniques by staging elaborate recreations of recent significant events. *Divers at Work on the Wreck of the 'Maine'* (1898) told of the sinking of the American battleship the Maine, the event which sparked the Spanish-American war. Méliès used a painted stage set of the underwater scene and had actors play the divers who rediscovered the wreck. A water-filled fishtank, placed in front of the camera through which the action was filmed, created the illusions of underwater filming, long before such a thing was actually possible. *The Dreyfuss Affair* (1899) told the story of the Jewish officer convicted of treason in 1894 on the basis of false evidence. When Méliès made his pro-Dreyfuss film, the controversy about the incident was still raging, five years after the events he depicted. Told in ten individual shots, the separate elements all had to be screened together one-after-the-other to gain the full impact of the complex story Méliès was attempting to tell. It was only with his next film, *Cinderella* (1899), which featured the famous story retold in 20 or so separate scenes, that Méliès joined the multiple shots together and was able to sell the film to exhibitors as one complete movie.

Rather than use actors or other performers in his earliest films, Méliès often appeared himself. After all, he knew exactly where he had to stand and what action he had to take to make his magical visual trickery work – and it saved having to explain it all to someone else. In *The Meloma-niac* (1903) Méliès played a character who could remove his own head, replace it with another and then toss the unwanted head up onto a telegraph wire. Perhaps revealing an obsession with heads, *The Man With the Rubber Head* (1902) similarly showed the director playing a character who could inflate his own head using an air pump, through clever use of double exposures.

Commerce and cinema cannot be separated. From its earliest days, the newest artform was a business, driven by technological development as much as artistic ambition. It's no surprise, then, to learn that many of Méliès' earliest films were actually advertisements promoting products, including Delion hats (in which rabbits turn into hats and back again – Méliès was ever the magician), Dewar's whisky, and a baldness cure (which featured Méliès himself applying the magical lotion to his bald head, which then sprouted copious locks).

For almost ten years, Méliès produced a series of ever more elaborate and ambitious films, pushing the boundaries of what could be achieved. Méliès' films proved extremely popular, sold well and were widely imitated by other filmmakers around the world. However, like many involved in the early days of cinema he suffered from financial problems caused by film piracy. Rather than buy his movies, unscrupulous distributors would simply make copies of them and then sell them on to exhibitors. As a result, Méliès was forced to open a sales office in the United States in 1903 (run by his brother Gaston) in an attempt to protect his financial interests. However he was very much a one-man band, and after 1905 Méliès found it harder to compete with larger film companies. As demand for movies grew, Méliès found he was unable to keep up the supply. The artisan was being replaced by the industrialist. As a sole creator of his films, he was rapidly eclipsed by the more industrialised film production business in the United States, despite joining Edison's Trust (the cartel Edison had set up, which was later declared illegal in 1915). In an attempt to meet the requirement that Trust members produce 1,000 feet of film every week to meet exhibitor demand, Méliès had Gaston set up an American unit to double his company's output. Initially based in New York, near Edison's studio, Gaston Méliès soon moved his outfit to San Antonio, Texas (where it shot mainly Westerns) before relocating again to an undeveloped region of southern California, later known as Hollywood...

Méliès continued to produce movies, including his late masterpiece *Conquest of the South Pole* (1912), but the nature of the movie business and indeed the nature of movies was changing in the middle years of the century's second decade. Méliès' work began to be perceived as somewhat old-fashioned as audience tastes matured and narrative sophistication grew. In 1912, deep in debt, Méliès ceased production, despite an unsatisfactory partnership with Pathé, having made just over 500 films (only a third of which are known to survive today).

Just before the outbreak of World War I, Méliès was forced to sell up his land holdings and he was eventually declared bankrupt in 1923, the same year his beloved Théâtre Robert-Houdin was demolished. By the mid-1920s, Méliès was back on his feet and had married one of his former film actresses, Jehanne d'Alcy (his first wife Eugenie having died in 1913). Together, they sold toys from a kiosk in the Gare Montparnasse until 1932, a pursuit far removed from the creation of bamboozling cinematic phantasmagoria, but one still arguably about giving pleasure to others. In 1931, Méliès was awarded the Cross of the Legion of Honour, ironically presented to him by Louis Lumière. His work was revived in the early 1930s as entertainment for children, while the French surrealists and film historians alike paid homage with visits to Méliès' retirement home in Orly. At the time of his death on 21 January 1938, Méliès was in discussion with Marcel Carné about making a film concerning a phantom on the Paris metro and a surrealistic retelling of the stories of Baron Munchausen.

Georges Méliès played a significantly pioneering role in the development of cinema, drawing upon his experiences in magical theatre to influence and anticipate the major developments of twentieth century filmmaking. Georges Méliès was an innovator and magical storyteller who did more than any other individual to make the illusion of cinema a reality.

THE DIRECTORS

In Europe and America, the new art form of cinema rapidly found an eager audience. The demand for films grew so quickly that it was often a struggle for the producers of filmed entertainment to keep up with the boom. Being silent, movies were an international business unhampered by problems of language. France, which dominated the international film market from 1906 to 1913, is often regarded as the home of many innovations in early cinema technique, especially in the work of screen magician Georges Méliès (see previous chapter), but others – both in France and beyond – developed the art of cinema and established the concept of the 'director' as the controller of what appeared on screen.

GEORGES MÉLIÈS (1861-1938)

See previous chapter

ALICE GUY-BLACHÉ (1875-1968)

Often overlooked in histories of early cinema, Alice Guy-Blaché was one of the new art form's earliest directors. She had begun her career as a secretary to Léon Gaumont. When his Gaumont company diversified from still photography into cinema, he needed someone to oversee the production of the films. Guy-Blaché is now recognised as the director of the world's first properly scripted drama, *The Cabbage Fairy/La Fée aux choux* (1896), which featured magical babies born in cabbage patches.

She was a pioneer, experimenting with sound, visual effects and special effects, such as painting directly onto celluloid film by hand. Many of her subsequent films drew upon Biblical stories for their inspiration. Guy-Blaché also founded one of the world's first proper film studios, Solax, in New York State, where she resided from 1907. It seems likely she directed hundreds of short films across many genres, including the classic American genre the Western and what would now be recognised as thrillers.

EDWIN STANTON (S.) PORTER (1869-1948)

Born in Pennsylvania, Edwin S. Porter began working in his 20s for a marketing company promoting the first American public screening of moving pictures by Edison at New York's Koster and Bial's Music Hall on 23 April 1896. Inspired, Porter joined Edison's company and began directing films, becoming one of the most important innovators in cinema. Initially confined to newsreel footage, Porter graduated to direct two significant films in 1903: *The Life of an American Fireman* and *The Great Train Robbery*. Trained as a cameraman, and someone for whom cinema was a series of technical challenges, Porter never really related his innovations to the 'art' of cinema. Although Méliès had pioneered many of the basic cinematic techniques, such as simple editing and the use of close-ups and developing continuity through editing, Porter also demonstrated – albeit in a cruder form – a grasp of the basic principles of cinematic continuity and narrative development. He never really developed them much further, though. Porter's editing consisted of 'parallel montage', cutting between two events happening simultaneously, rather than 'continuity editing' in which relationships (such as point-of-view) are built between shots cut together.

The Life of an American Fireman cuts between the arrival of a fireman outside a blazing house and the events going on in the interior of the house, where the fireman rescues a mother-and-child. Cutting to the street outside where the rescued mother waits for her child to be retrieved, the film uses cutting not only to show the sequence of events, but to create tension in the characters and so in the audience. Mere thrills were not enough any more, audiences wanted to be emotionally engaged by the films they watched and Porter was one of the filmmakers who began the process of developing the 'film language' necessary to achieve that engagement. The simple but effective editing of *The Great Train Robbery* tells that particular story well, but that was the limit of it for Porter. He was good with group action, but his work does little to develop individual characters.

Similarly his later films, such as *Uncle Tom's Cabin* (1910) and *Life of an American Policeman* (1905), suffer from the same problems. Porter's focus was on plot, not people, and his rudimentary editing skills were more often used in pursuit of simple storytelling rather than emotional engagement. Actors – even in his later feature films – seem to have been incidental to Porter. Although hailed as an innovator – and his subsequent career saw him experimenting with sound, widescreen films, colour and even 3D movies – Porter's failure to fulfil his early promise and to further develop film aesthetics has relegated him to the position of a cinematic 'also-ran', rapidly superseded by those who immediately followed him. As with so many others, Porter was bankrupted by the 1929 Wall Street Crash, and died, largely forgotten by history, in 1948.

Edwin Porter's *Rescued From an Eagle's Nest* (1907), a melodrama about an eagle's kidnap of a baby and its subsequent rescue, is primarily notable for one thing: the appearance of actor (soon to turn innovative director) David Wark Griffith among the cast...

DAVID WARK (DW) GRIFFITH (1875-1948)

A modestly successful playwright and sometime actor, DW Griffith was born in Kentucky in 1875. His Confederate officer father died when Griffith was ten. Involved in amateur theatre in his twenties, Griffith approached the Edison company hoping to break into films. Much like Porter before him, many of the innovations in basic cinematic language are attributed to Griffith, but with more justification. Griffith then worked for Edison rival Biograph, starting as an actor but soon moving behind the camera in 1908, directing hundreds of one- and two-reel films over the next half decade. Unlike Porter, Griffith was particularly effective with actors (partly due to his own theatrical background, something he shared with Méliès). He was also good at adapting theatrical devices to film (again, as with Méliès), particularly in terms of the dramatic use of lighting. He effectively used and developed such techniques as the close-up, panning and tracking the camera, and Porter's parallel editing. He succeeded where Porter had failed in creating films that emotionally engaged the audience, rather than just depicting situations. Griffith drew largely on a story form with which his audiences would be familiar: the Victorian melodrama. While that allowed Griffith to directly connect with audiences, it was hardly an innovative form and certainly not unique to cinema. Other filmmakers, such as Mack Sennett – who worked for Griffith as an actor and writer – would go on to develop story forms (in his case the slapstick chase film) unique to cinema, leaving Griffith trapped in old-time melodramatics. Even at the start of his film career, Griffith was looking backwards, while others like Sennett were willing to explore the new medium in a much more forward looking way.

Griffith made more than 450 films at Biograph, often in collaboration with cameraman GW (Billy) Blitzer. The sheer volume of work allowed for the stylistic experimentation that would result in the development of a basic film language that all subsequent commercial filmmakers would adopt as standard. He moved cinema from the static, tableaux-like staging of scenes (inherited from the proscenium arch limitations of theatre) towards a freer, more fluid form that set loose the camera to explore the three-dimensional space of the real world. He built on Porter's initial forays into editing to break up scenes into a series of shots taken from a variety of angles and distances, combined in such a way that emphasised the emotional content of the action, rather than merely *depicting* the action. His work with actors, drawn from the stage, resulted in what is now seen as a ridiculously over-the-top, terribly theatrical style of declarative

The Birth of a Nation (1915)

acting. Yet in the early days of film, this was deemed necessary to communicate character's feelings clearly to an audience for whom this was all new. He also developed the idea of rehearsing scenes with his actors before going on to shoot them.

Griffith's cinematic triumphs were *The Birth of a Nation* (1915) and *Intolerance* (1916), as well as *Broken Blossoms* (1919). Building on the cross-cutting of *The Lonely Villa* (1909), Griffith refined his techniques in further kidnap or race-against-time melodramas, such as *The Fatal Hour* (1908), *Her Terrible Ordeal* (1910) and *The Lonedale Operator* (1911). Each film featured precise editing, but lacked dramatic camera movement. So successful in establishing a recognisable style was Griffith that critics of the time often talked of other films being 'up to' or 'below' Biograph standards, or of using 'Biograph lighting'. Much of Griffith's work prefigured the developments of later European directors. *The Musketeers of Pig Alley* (1912) anticipated the montage of Eisenstein a decade later, while *An Unseen Enemy* (1912) captured a surreal, nightmare quality that would be at home in the later French cliff-hanger serials of Feuillade. Griffith's use of close-ups and repeated use of key actresses and actors would ultimately lead to the development of the star system (see Chapter 6: The Dramatic Stars).

It was Griffith who would spearhead the move away from one- and two-reel films to epic 'feature' length productions. Again, the driver was audience attraction: an epic was something special that could attract big crowds and justify a higher ticket price, thus keeping exhibitors happy too. His first four-reel feature was *Judith of Bethulia* (1913), the release of which was delayed by Biograph and the studio's distributor, the General Film Company. This resulted in Griffith moving on to work for Reliance Majestic (later Mutual), where he became Head of Production. His work there led on to his adaptation of Thomas Dixon's novel *The Clansman*, released as *The Birth of a Nation*. This family saga set during the American civil war was a sensation. Griffith brought everything he'd learned in seven years of filmmaking to this still-controversial movie. He followed the original source material, uncritically glorifying the southern states' racist organisation the Ku Klux Klan, resulting in a revival for the organisation that had disbanded in 1869.

Having paved the way for the adoption of the feature film as a standard, Griffith's ambition knew no bounds. The result was the largely self-financed grand production of *Intolerance* (1916), which ran for a total of three-and-a-quarter hours. Although much of what Griffith achieved in *Intolerance* would influence subsequent filmmaking, the movie was met with mystification and – worse – indifference, resulting in huge financial problems for its director. While he continued to work, Griffith never really recovered from the failure of *Intolerance*. He was involved in founding United Artists with Chaplin, Pickford and Fairbanks, but was a subdued partner in the enterprise. Even before the coming of sound, Griffith's films were seen as old-fashioned: he was a mere spectator as the 1930s saw a consolidation of all he had pioneered. An innovator in the art form, Griffith had freed American cinema from its primitive technical limitations and reliance on theatrical influence. It would be left to others to develop the narrative side of cinema building on Griffith's solid foundations.

CECIL BLOUNT (B.) DEMILLE (1881-1959)

It was to director Cecil B. DeMille that the development of cinematic storytelling fell. DeMille's father was a preacher much drawn to amateur dramatics, and the son inherited the father's flare for performance. A spell at military college preceded DeMille's arrival at the Academy of Dramatic Arts. Acting and writing followed, before DeMille hooked up with Jesse Lasky and Samuel Goldfish (later Goldwyn) in 1913, formed the Lasky Feature Play Company and travelled to an obscure town named Hollywood to shoot DeMille's first feature film, *The Squaw Man* (1914). They were not the first to shoot movies in that quiet Californian hamlet, but their arrival caused many more film pioneers to follow, resulting in the growth of Hollywood as the film industry town. By 1918, Lasky's company had merged with Adolph Zukor's Famous Players to form

Paramount, the studio for which DeMille would mainly work, ushering in the earliest beginning of the Hollywood studio system.

DeMille built upon and expanded the techniques developed by Griffith, especially in the areas of dramatic lighting and set designs. He made many historic 'costume pictures', although he roamed from genre to genre. *The Woman God Forgot* (1919) was a romantic tale focused around religious conflict, while a series of witty romantic comedies starring Gloria Swanson (including *Male and Female* [1919]) followed. While he later gained a reputation for overblown epics, DeMille's storytelling skills were evident in his earliest work. He realised, in a way that went beyond the work of Porter and Griffith, that for a film to truly succeed it had to emotionally involve the audience with the characters and events depicted on screen. DeMille also realised the importance of the audience connecting his name with a certain type of film: he was a showman on and off screen, resulting in the megaphone wielding, jodhpur wearing caricature of an early Hollywood director (see also Erich von Stroheim). In giving the audience what they want and making each movie a promotable event, DeMille had invented Hollywood...

MACK SENNETT (MIKALL SINNOTT) (1880-1960)

From his background in burlesque and the Broadway chorus, it seemed clear that Canadian-born, Irish-descended Mack Sennett was not cut out for dramatic filmmaking. He learned basic film techniques from DW Griffith from 1908 at Biograph, where he met future partner and screen star Mabel Normand. After trying his hand at acting, Sennett was directing at Biograph from 1910. He and Normand quit to set up Keystone in 1912, the only studio solely devoted to the production of comedy shorts. Over the first year, the studio's output quickly established the Keystone formula: a series of eccentric characters caught up in strange goings on which climaxed in a wild chase sequence. It was simple, easy to do and certainly audience pleasing. Shooting in and around the slowly developing suburban areas of Los Angeles, Sennett's films had a ready-made backdrop. Most were shot, rough-and-ready, on location giving an added verisimilitude to the comic happenings and capturing a moment in time before Los Angeles became the urban sprawl it is today. Although most of the Keystone films began with a script, or at least a scenario, Sennett was not above abandoning what he was shooting to include something found on location, whether a passing parade or a suitable comic building.

Established as the top studio in its genre by 1913, Sennett surrounded himself with a handful of other directors who followed closely the trademark studio style he'd established. On screen talent joining Mabel Normand consisted of Mack Swain, Chester Conklin and Roscoe 'Fatty' Arbuckle, who'd starred in the first of the Keystone Kops films. By the end of 1913, Charlie Chaplin joined Sennett's set-up at Keystone for a year. When Chaplin objected to the directors he was assigned, Sennett personally took over until Chaplin assumed control over his own output. Sennett would also occasionally indulge himself with continued on-screen appearances, as in *Mabel's Dramatic Career* (1913) and playing himself in *The Hollywood Kid* (1924). As time went on, Sennett directed less, having established the technique of silent comedy shorts. Many others were imitating the Keystone style, while some of his best technicians were defecting to newly formed companies set up to rival Keystone.

Sennett became more of a mini-mogul, emphasising the growing importance of the producer in the film business, merging his company with those of DW Griffith and Thomas H. Ince to create the Triangle Film Corporation in 1915. Later, under his own name, Sennett would move into feature films, starring Ben Turpin among others. By the 1920s, he was championing the work of Harry Langdon. The coming of sound saw Sennett returning to directing, helming some WC Fields shorts at Paramount and others featuring a young Bing Crosby.

Bankrupt by 1933, Sennett was awarded an honorary Oscar in 1938 in recognition of his work in silent film comedy. Keystone remains to this day as lazy shorthand for all silent comedy, especially those involving chases or physical slapstick, whether made by Mack Sennett or not.

THE DRAMATIC STARS

When cinema began there were no movie stars. The biggest star – in the sense of being well known by the public – of early cinema was one of the medium's founding fathers: Thomas Alva Edison. Other areas of performance – theatre, opera, and even the 'low' entertainment of vaudeville – operated on a recognised 'star system', but the nascent cinema industry either didn't see the attraction of such a focus, or – more often – deliberately avoided it.

The earliest actors in cinema went without credit, often being named after the company who produced the film. The earliest silent cinema stars were the likes of 'the Biograph girl' and 'the Vitagraph girl'.

It was the cinema audiences who made stars of the mostly anonymous performers up on the screen. It was their desire to put names to the faces they were beginning to recognise in film after film that brought about the first proper 'movie stars', actors and actresses whose names would become familiar to the audience and whose appearance in a film was enough to draw them to the cinema. Film fan magazines began to publish profiles of the actors and actresses who were making it in films in Hollywood. One of the earliest references to a screen actor being dubbed a 'star' came in a photo caption in the June 1910 edition of *The New York Dramatic Mirror*, which dubbed 'Vitagraph girl' Florence Turner a 'motion picture star'.[3] At the time, Turner was 'starring' as the lead in a movie with the dry title of *A Tin-Type Romance* (1910). Florence was to fulfil the tragic trajectory that would befall many movie stars: she committed suicide in 1938 by consuming insect poison.

Two actors in particular came to represent the new 'star system' of Hollywood: Mary Pickford and Douglas Fairbanks, the first superstar celebrity couple of the movies. They took to the new medium like naturals and their marriage made them the first members of a new entertainment dynasty: the movie stars. Movie stardom was a different level of fame from any that had preceded the age of cinema. Film fans felt a kind of 'ownership' of 'their' film stars. The movies (and so the stars) came to the audience, playing in their local cinemas. The huge images (close-ups of their faces) were projected onto giant screens, searing themselves into the minds of audiences. Their identities became fixed through the roles they played: more often than not they fulfilled 'types' or archetypes. The audience were drawn into direct and close relationships with the actors who played the characters on screen. Lack of language barriers resulted in the first generation of movie stars becoming internationally famous in a way that simply doesn't exist today. Stardom was democratic and access was affordable, even to those of limited means. The actors were special, yet ordinary – just like their fans. Whether that was true or just another illusion, movie stars entered the imagination and the dreams of the audience.

MARY PICKFORD (1892-1979)

One of cinemas earliest 'ingénues', Pickford was born Gladys Marie Smith in 1892 (some sources suggest 1893) in Toronto, Canada – a Canadian who became one of the American film business' earliest name 'stars'. She was also one of the earliest cinema practitioners, whether behind or in front of the camera, to realise their own burgeoning power within the industry. Her father was killed when she was five or six, and the resultant financial pressures on the family meant her mother had to let rooms in their home, often to actors. It was through this early exposure to acting as a profession that Pickford found her way to cinema via the stage and so to her screen persona of 'Little Mary', the perpetual 'little girl' in a confusing, grown-up world.

Mary Pickford

In 1909, DW Griffith engaged Pickford at Biograph, where she was known initially as 'the Biograph girl' and remained – learning the basics of screen craft and the organisation of this new industry – until 1912. She made 75 two-reelers (42 alone in 1909, a mere 32 in 1910) with Griffith, becoming one of his biggest stars in the process.

Showing her business acumen, she'd briefly left Griffith in 1910 for a short stint at Independent Pictures, managing to twice increase her salary in the process. She started writing scenarios for her films, for which she earned additional income. By 1913, she was working at Zukor's Famous Players studio, earning the unheard of sum of $500 per week. By 1916 she'd eclipsed that, earning $10,000 every week, such was her proven box office popularity.[4] Despite the fact that they had a turbulent working relationship, it was Griffith who'd dubbed Pickford's screen character 'Little Mary'. She later had a similar tempestuous time working on two films with Cecil B. DeMille (1917's gold rush drama *A Romance of the Redwoods* and the wartime-set *The Little American*). It was her time with Zukor, though, that saw the actress enshrine her sentimental persona, her popularity and her business acumen. Popular in comedy and melodrama, it's the latter that are remembered today, obscuring the fact that in many ways Pickford was the female Charlie Chaplin. She played a wide range of roles, serious, tragic and comic, becoming an audience favourite in the process.

Pickford's directors – including Edwin S. Porter on 1913's *Hearts Adrift* and 1914's *Tess of the Storm Country*, James Kirkwood on 1914's *Cinderella* (a signature role for Pickford), and Allan Dwan on 1915's *The Foundling* – were more often directed by her, rather than the other way around. She proved to be an excellent judge of her own appeal to audiences and so a great selector of her own material, in terms of scripts and roles. In *Rags* (1915) she even managed to play two roles: a mother and her daughter. This was to become a habit: she tackled two very different roles in *Stella Maris* (1918) and played both the male title character and his mother in *Little Lord Fauntleroy* (1921)! During World War I, Pickford was the 'Forces sweetheart', touring the country to sell war bonds to raise finance to fund the army, while still making a series of blockbusting films with directors Maurice Tourneur, Cecil B. DeMille, and William Desmond Taylor.

By 1919, she was enjoying complete creative control over her films at First National, but still splitting the profits with the studio. Shortly thereafter, she joined with Charlie Chaplin, Douglas Fairbanks and Griffith in establishing their own studio, United Artists. This would give her ultimate control of her own films, from production to distribution. After the end of her first marriage with actor Owen Moore, she married Fairbanks – one of cinema's first great showbusiness romances, reported in all the fan magazines. Still 'America's sweetheart', Pickford entered her 30s more powerful than ever before. However, in order to maintain her audience appeal she insisted on continuing to appear adolescent on screen, resulting in a series of challenges for her lighting cameramen. She found one in particular, Charles Rosher, who was up to the task of creating the on-screen illusion of endless adolescence. Even this early in cinema history, longevity in the business seemed dependent upon youth and beauty, no matter how artificially maintained.

In 1923, Pickford brought Ernst Lubitsch to America from Germany to handle her movies, but their alliance soon faltered. By the end of the silent era, and with the coming of sound, movies were changing, as were audience tastes. Although she made a few sound films and worked in movies until 1933, Pickford took a positive decision to end her acting career at the age of 41. Her final silent film was 1927's *My Best Girl*, which paired her with her third and final husband Charles 'Buddy' Rogers. She would win an Oscar for best actress in her first sound film, 1929's *Coquette*. However, unable to maintain the illusion of youth for much longer, as cinematic acting styles changed around her, Pickford seemed unable to learn anew or to adapt to the new styles. She continued to work producing films into the 1940s, and in 1953 she and Chaplin sold their shares in United Artists. 'I left the screen because I didn't want what happened to Chaplin to happen to me... The little girl made me, I wasn't waiting for the little girl to kill me,' she said.[5]

Contemporary Equivalent: Early Julia Roberts.

Douglas Fairbanks, *Don Q, Son of Zorro* (1925)

DOUGLAS FAIRBANKS (1883-1939)

Born a decade before Pickford, as Douglas Elton Ulman in Denver, Colorado, Douglas Fairbanks became one of cinema's earliest swashbuckling heroes. He, along with Mary Pickford and Charlie Chaplin, were the first true 'movie stars'. Fairbanks virtually invented the swashbuckling action adventure movie hero, and he's rarely been bettered on screen. A star on stage before the movies, Fairbanks made his debut in 1915 in *The Lamb*, having decided that the stage could not contain his epic storytelling ambitions. Like Pickford, Fairbanks was not content just to act and was determined to take control of his films. Along with directors John Emerson and Allan Dwan, he left Triangle to form his own production company. By 1919, he was one of the four founders of United Artists, marrying Pickford in 1920. Some believe that some of Pickford's dramatic action scenes actually feature Fairbanks in a wig and a cloak, doubling for his wife.

As a producer on his own action epics, he was inclined to take the business aspects of film production as seriously as he did the acting: after all, it was his investment he was protecting. Historical accuracy obsessed him, as did the need to convince an audience, which often led to the actor doing his own stunts. Fairbanks played trademark heroic figures in *The Mark of Zorro* (1920), *The Three Musketeers* (1921), *Robin Hood* (1922), *The Thief of Bagdad* (1924) and *The Black Pirate* (1926). He embodied every kid's desire to dress up and play make-believe, whether as Zorro, Robin Hood, a Musketeer or a pirate... Despite his audience popularity, Fairbanks found the transition to sound films difficult. He only completed a handful of sound movies, before ending his marriage to Pickford in 1935 and retiring from the screen just as she had.

Contemporary Equivalent: Russell Crowe crossed with Indiana Jones-era Harrison Ford.

MABEL NORMAND (1894-1930)

Known familiarly by audiences as simply 'Mabel', like contemporary star 'Madonna', Normand was the pin-up star of the Keystone comedy movies, often seen alongside comedians like Charlie Chaplin and Fatty Arbuckle in the years leading up to World War I. Born just after Mary Pickford, in Boston, Massachusetts, Normand was one of the first 'stars' of the cinema who had no real experience in acting and didn't pretend on screen to be anyone other than herself, dropped into one madcap situation after another. She'd been a model before signing up with DW Griffith at Biograph in 1911. She was only 16, but she featured prominently in several Griffith movies, such as 1911's *The Squaw's Love*. However, it was with director Mack Sennett at Biograph that she had the most success. She became his female attraction of choice to offset the resolute maleness of his comedy shorts. When Sennett quit Biograph to set up Keystone in 1912, he took Normand with him and the pair worked closely together until 1917. By the age of 20, in 1914, Normand was directing her own films, and her 'Mabel' character often featured in the titles. These simple titles not only promoted 'Mabel' as a star figure, they also served as plot descriptions outlining the situation of each two-reeler: *Mabel's New Job*; *Mabel's Latest Prank*; *Mabel at the Wheel*; *Mabel's Stormy Love Affair* and *Mabel's Blunder*.

Normand and Chaplin had a falling out when Chaplin petitioned Sennett to be allowed to write and direct his own material, only to find himself assigned Normand as his director instead. Chaplin doubted Normand's competence and he refused to take her direction. Although they did work together again, Normand was to find more success teamed up with Fatty Arbuckle in 1915. Arbuckle was starring in and directing his own comedies, and he shared title billing with Normand in such films as *Mabel and Fatty's Wash Day*; *Fatty and Mabel's Simple Life*; *Fatty and Mabel at the San Diego Exposition*; and *Mabel, Fatty and the Law*, among many others.

Normand wanted to move into feature films, something not possible at Sennett's studio that produced only shorts, so she switched to Paramount for 1918's *Mickey*. Building a career as a well-loved film actress, Mabel Normand seemed on a roll through the post-war years, until 1922. She was caught up in the scandal of the murder of film director William Desmond Taylor (see Chapter 8: Silent Scandals for the full story) and found her career on the slide. She returned to Sennett to no avail and ended up making her final shorts for Laurel & Hardy producer Hal Roach in 1926, before dying a mere four years later at the age of 36 (the same age as Marilyn Monroe and Princess Diana at their deaths).

Contemporary Equivalent: Meg Ryan.

WILLIAM S. HART (1870-1946) & TOM MIX (1880-1940)

In the early days of cinema, real life cowboys were able to bring their unique expertise direct to the screen. In the late 1880s, William S. Hart had taken part in real cattle drives and worked in a riding school, so he certainly knew his way around a horse. Hart found a new, and very different, career as a stage actor between 1890 and 1910, achieving some success in a Broadway production of *Ben-Hur*. It's likely he would have ended up in movies eventually, but it was his friendship with cinema pioneer Thomas H. Ince that brought Hart to the screen quicker than may otherwise have happened. Thus was born cinema's first cowboy hero... Often playing reformed outlaws, Hart brought maturity to the cowboy as befitting his middle-years... Inspired by Ince's example, Hart swiftly moved behind the camera, writing and directing the films in which he starred from about 1917 to around 1919, including *The Silent Man* (1917), *The Narrow Trail* (1917), *The Border Wireless* (1918) and *Shark Monroe* (1918). For most of the early 1920s, however, Hart performed under the direction of Ince protégé Lambert Hillyer, who helmed *Wagon Tracks* (1919) and *The Cradle of Courage* (1920), among many others. In 1923, Hart played in Famous Player's production of *Wild Bill Hickok* (1923) before retiring from the screen in 1925, after co-directing his final film *Tumbleweeds* (1925).

Almost exactly paralleling Hart was Tom Mix, another of the silent era's cowboy heroes. Like Hart, Mix found his way into movies on the back of his undoubted way with horses. Born in Pennsylvania to a lumberjack father, Mix was in the army, then the Texas Rangers, before performing in a Wild West show in 1906, turning the recent real-life West into formulaic entertainment for city folks. Hired initially to look after the horses in films, Mix soon graduated to stunt work and then to leading man status. From 1910 onwards, Mix was acting in the movies making a series of disposable single and double-reeler Westerns. By 1917, he was working at Fox and taking control of his own output, directing his own work just as Hart did. Aware of the importance of image to the potential impact of a movie star, Mix went to great lengths to cultivate an instantly recognisable Western look for himself. He took Hart's 'authentic' approach one step further, offering a series of thrills and adventures which may not have reflected the real West in the way that Hart was endeavouring to do, but offered far more in the way of entertainment. More of an instinctive showman than the more reserved Hart, Tom Mix was the number one cowboy movie star of the 1920s, turning out up to half-a-dozen films each year, one every couple of months. Mix even survived the coming of sound, continuing for a few years in the early 1930s to make more movies. Following his death (in a car crash in 1940) the image Mix had cultivated lived on, as a character in radio serials and portrayed in comic books. Tom Mix was the truly iconic cowboy star of the silent era.

Contemporary Equivalent: Bruce Willis.

GLORIA SWANSON (1897-1983)

Perhaps better known today for her turn as Norma Desmond, the over-the-hill diva of Billy Wilder's *Sunset Boulevard* (1950), Chicago-born Gloria Swanson had actually been one of the most successful and certainly one of the most highly paid stars of the silent era, after Chaplin. While she may have been willing to play off perceptions of her own image, following her retirement from movies in 1934, Swanson's own silent career did not mirror that of Norma Desmond. Coming from an army family, the young Swanson started in the movies at the age of 17, winning a job at the Essanay Studios in Chicago, which also provided an outlet for Charlie Chaplin. In 1915, she married co-star Wallace Beery and headed west to Hollywood, appearing in a variety of Mack Sennett two-reel comedies. By 1918, she had moved on to Triangle before signing with Cecil B. DeMille in 1919. A series of moralising melodramas followed, with her making a run of drama-driven films in New York in the early 1920s. Like many stars of the silent era, Swanson was out to wrest control of her own career from those running the studios. She began selecting her own material, which resulted in a move into comedy in the mid-1920s. Forming her own production company, with a distribution deal through United Artists, Swanson made *Queen Kelly* (1928), still one of her best-known films due to the problems that surrounded it. A tale of sexual adventure directed by Erich von Stroheim (her butler in *Sunset Boulevard*), *Queen Kelly* was re-edited by its star to try and create a more marketable film after the director was fired. Swanson failed and the picture was never released in the US, leaving Swanson in debt until she made *Sunset Boulevard* in

1950. There were other more successful films produced by and starring Swanson, but she quit the screen in 1934 claiming that the times were out of step with her. Following *Sunset Boulevard*, she appeared in a handful of films, including *Airport 1975* (1974) as herself, before once more retiring from the limelight.

Contemporary Equivalent: Jodie Foster.

RUDOLPH VALENTINO (1895-1926)

Known simply as 'Valentino' to his fans, Rodolpho Guglielmi di Valentina d'Antonguolla sensibly changed his name to Rudolph Valentino, setting a precedent that many Europeans making their way in Hollywood would later emulate. Born in Castellaneta in Italy, a couple of years after Mabel Normand, Valentino would become the romantic poster boy of silent cinema. Dubbed 'the screen's greatest lover',[6] Valentino was the cinema's first sex symbol, whose dozen or so movies etched an unforgettable image of fey masculinity in the minds and libidos of audiences of the 1920s. He was never a straightforward romantic hero, projecting an image of dangerous sexuality only tamed by the frame of the cinema screen in films such as *The Four Horsemen of the Apocalypse* (1921), *Uncharted Seas* (1921), *Camille* (1921) and *The Conquering Power* (1921). The all-conquering image of Valentino was, however – and remains – that of *The Sheik* (1921). As an Arab who captures a 'spirited English girl', Valentino seems inclined to take the woman by force rather than romance and seduction, until he is wounded and nursed back to health by her. Only then is he converted to the thought that marriage might be the way to go... The potency of the Valentino image cannot be doubted, though it is very easy to mock today. It's one of the earliest examples of a 'star' image being created and consumed, and becoming bigger and more influential than the mere actor who spawned it in the first place. In *The Sheik*, Valentino offered a kind of forbidden glamour, an escape from mundanity (the foundation of so much of cinema). Yet, his taming into marriage also offered a kind of reassurance that 'normality' would prevail over the wild

Rudolph Valentino and Vilma Banky, *Son of the Sheik* (1926)

fantasy of the untamed. For many critics Valentino was no actor (much like 'ordinary girl' Mabel Normand) but was simply a poseur of the first order. At this stage of cinema's development, this was enough to ignite audience frenzy and create a star image that, much like real celestial stars, was fated to burn out rather than fade away.

Valentino had lived the American dream, rising from shady beginnings to conquer the nation, only to exit the stage at the height of his power. He'd arrived in America in 1914, and had worked as a dancer (hence the source of accusations that he was little more than a 'gigolo'), a movie extra and had even resorted to theft in order to survive. Had he been a male prostitute, too? These rumours and questions about 'the great lover's' sexuality only served to add to his mystique and fuel his cinematic ambivalence. Dubbed 'the Pink Powder Puff' in the press[7], Valentino's feminised image was beginning to catch up with him as he dominated such films as *Beyond the Rocks* (1922) with Gloria Swanson, *Blood and Sand* (1922) as a bullfighter, *The Eagle* (1925) and *The Son of the Sheik* (1925). As the first movie star to appeal to women and men, Valentino was a pioneer, but scandal loomed. He was thrust into myth, and saved from probable humiliation in sound films, by his untimely death in 1926. He collapsed in New York that summer and was rushed to hospital, diagnosed with an inoperable case of peritonitis. His funeral drew huge, grieving crowds to the streets, stopping traffic and providing a spectacle only Hollywood could create. If Valentino achieved one thing above all others, it was the art of dying young as a cinematic career move (later emulated by others, specifically James Dean and River Phoenix).

Contemporary Equivalent: Leonardo DiCaprio (at the height of *Titanic* mania), with a dash of Johnny Depp, a slice of Brad Pitt and a soupçon of Will Smith...

LOUISE BROOKS (1906-1985)

Louise Brooks is a bigger star now than she ever was during the silent movie age. A pin-up and icon of silent movie sexuality, Brooks is perhaps

Louise Brooks

more famous now for her bobbed hairstyle than for her film roles. The mystique of Louise Brooks, read into her image rather than from her films, is so much larger than her actual achievements – something the actress herself cultivated cleverly in her years of retirement. Brooks, born Mary Louise Brooks in Kansas, found her way into the movies through dancing and bit parts in disposable comedies. She played *femme fatale* characters long before film noir became a recognised genre, luring men to their doom. The mid-1920s saw her busy American period, churning out *The American Venus* (1926), *It's the Old Army Game* (1926, alongside W. C. Fields and directed by Edward Sutherland, briefly married to Brooks), *Just Another Blonde* (1926), *Rolled Stockings* (1927), and Howard Hawks' *A Girl in Every Port* (1928).

Then something quite unlikely happened: Brooks went to Europe, breaking her contract with Paramount, to pursue her artistic muse. G.W. Pabst found Brooks through *A Girl in Every Port* and signed her up as Lulu in his *Pandora's Box* (1929), which became her iconic role. The 23-year-old found herself in Germany, shooting *Pandora's Box* and *Diary of a Lost Girl* (1929). Having burnt her bridges in Hollywood, she ended up featuring in French film *Prix de Beauté* (1930), before returning to Los Angeles and appearing in a two-reeler comedy directed by the then-disgraced Fatty Arbuckle. The sound era saw the end of Brooks' career, although it had nothing to do with her vocal abilities. Having turned her back on Hollywood, the film industry in turn gave her short shrift upon her return. By 1938, she was out of the movies. Her legend, however, was secure, and she became a real-life Norma Desmond, trading on her past.

Contemporary Equivalent: Madonna, perhaps, or Jennifer Jason Leigh.

LILLIAN GISH (1893-1993)

Lillian Gish proved to be one of the longest living of all the silent era movie stars, working right up until the late 1980s, having achieved what next to none of her contemporaries managed: a career which not only survived the coming of sound but positively thrived across the century of her life. She was one of the first movie stars and one of the last connections to that lost, magical time when the movies began. She was in *Birth of a Nation* (1915) and *Intolerance* (1916), the two silent movies everyone has heard of. She spanned the period from the Victorian to the Reagan Years, when movies 'developed' from her appearance in *Broken Blossoms* (1919) to the cinema of Rambo, Rocky and the Terminator.

Abandoned by their father, Lillian Gish and her sister Dorothy (1898-1968) joined a travelling theatre. Visiting Mary Pickford, a family friend, in 1912, the pair was persuaded into the movies by DW Griffith. Gish appeared in over 20 two-reelers for Griffith until making the new medium's first four-reeler, *Judith of Bethulia* (1913). She followed Griffith, working with him in *The Battle of the Sexes* (1914), *The Escape* (1914), *Home Sweet Home* (1914) and *The Birth of a Nation* (1915). Audiences, and Gish herself, came to closely associate her screen persona with the films of Griffith, although she did work with other directors in the late-teens. More Griffith films followed in the years either side of 1920, including *Hearts of the World* (1918) and the character of the archetypal East End waif in *Broken Blossoms*. She appeared with her sister Dorothy in Griffith's *Orphans of the Storm* (1921) and directed her sister in *Remodelling Her Husband* (1920).

Gish and Griffith parted ways in 1921 over a financial dispute, though Gish continued to talk highly of her main director for the rest of her life, entitling her eventual autobiography, *The Movies, Mr Griffith and Me*. A strange pseudo-scandal followed when she sued the head of a studio she was working at who'd claimed she'd reneged on a promise to marry him and won. Signed to MGM for six films at a fee of $800,000, Gish spent the late-1920s battling a studio management who wanted to sex her up to match public tastes. Arranged scandals were offered and refused, with Gish determined to exercise the power her contract gave her over her own material. Her best films resulted, including *La Bohème* (1926), *The Scarlet Letter* (1926) and *The Wind* (1928), her greatest melodrama. Her MGM contract over, Gish departed with her head held high. She made some more films in the early sound years, before opting for theatre over cinema. The 1940s then saw a return to films, and she played distinguished character roles through the 1950s and 1960s. She worked with Robert Altman in 1978 in *A Wedding*, and was still acting for film in her 80s, through to *The Whales of August* (1987) for Lindsay Anderson. Her will stipulated that when she died – as eventually happened in March 1993, mere months shy of her hundredth birthday – that her money should go to The Museum of Modern Art expressly for the task of preserving the work of DW Griffith.

Contemporary Equivalent: Gwyneth Paltrow.

MARION DAVIES (1897-1961)

Appreciated more as the mistress of publishing tycoon William Randolph Hearst and as the inspiration for the kept opera singer wife Susan Alexander in Orson Welles' *Citizen Kane* (1940), Marion Davies is barely thought of as a silent movie actress of any note these days. More often the answer to a trivia question concerning the meaning of 'Rosebud', Davies in fact enjoyed a significant and notable career on the screen.

Marion Cecilia Douras was born in New York and came to fame via the Ziegfeld Follies dance troupe, where she met Hearst. She was with him for the better part of 30 years, until his death in 1951. Hearst was determined to make her dreams of film stardom come true, forming a film company purely for her. By 1919 her films were finding an audience thanks to a distribution deal with Paramount and it seemed that Davies' forte was for knock-about comedy, popular at the time. Hearst, however, felt that it would be more befitting someone of her (and his) status to appear in costumed historical melodramas, rather than the kind of film where his mistress was likely to get a custard pie thrust in her face. Davies was singularly unsuited to such roles, but Hearst had the money, the power and her heart.

A new alliance with MGM saw Davies receiving special treatment way out of alignment with her worth as a minor movie star, but which MGM's

LB Mayer saw as worthwhile to keep the free publicity in Hearst's news-papers coming. Hearst wielded the kind of economic power that could make or break not only individual films, but entire studios, as shown by his paper's boycott of Welles' *Citizen Kane*, which intimately parodied not only Davies but Hearst himself. Backed by Hearst and her favour-seeking studio, Davies made the transition to sound easily enough, before dropping out of films in the late-1930s, her indulgence sated. She spent her final years loyally looking after a much diminished Hearst and didn't return to the screen.

Contemporary Equivalent: Demi Moore.

LON CHANEY (1883-1930)

Known as 'the man of a thousand faces', Lon Chaney was a master of movie magic. He made cinematic transformation an art form, not merely content to use make-up and illusion to create fantastical characters, but willing to contort his whole body to inhabit each distinctive character. As the child of deaf and mute parents, Colorado-born Alonso Chaney became used to acting out tales of his own activities for his parents' benefit. His childhood also gave Chaney a keen insight into the suffering that was possible in ordinary life. Chaney's entry into showbusiness was as a 'travelling player', taking his acrobatics and vaudeville-type act around America's major emerging cities.

By 1912, he was in Los Angeles and found work at Universal Studios, where he was able to put his make-up box, which was constantly with him, to fine use. It has been suggested that he may have used his make-up skills to disguise himself in real life, either to escape the law or the Mob, but now he had the opportunity to put his skills to use entertaining others. His first roles were as simple thugs – the muscle, the henchman – to the movie's bad guy. Often, through his make-up skills, he would play multiple parts in a single movie. He made in excess of 70 movies at Universal between 1913 and 1917, many of them now lost. As with so many silent films, the titles tell the audience much about the kind of film they're about

Lon Chaney

to see: *Red Margaret – Moonshiner* (1913), *Discord and Harmony* (1913), *The Embezzler* (1913), *The Threads of Fate* (1915), *Grasp of Greed* (1916) and *The Mark of Cain* (1917).

Film stardom so often depended upon an actor or actress being easily recognisable from film to film and often playing variations on the same part, time and time again. Lon Chaney was the antithesis of this: in every film he was very different, looking different and acting different. It was for this versatility that he was finally recognised by the public, playing a San Francisco gangster at the time of the 1906 earthquake in *Hell Morgan's Girl* (1917). Chaney's stardom came to rely upon the way he could change his face, manipulate his image and be distinctive in every film. Working with maverick director Tod Browning, Chaney found his métier. He was in Browning's *The Wicked Darling* (1919) and *Outside the Law* (1921) – in which he played a gangster and a Chinaman, affording him the opportunity to shoot himself – before playing his signature role as the title character in *The Hunchback of Notre Dame* (1923). He was stunning as a criminal disguised as a helpless old woman in Tod Browning's *The Unholy Three* (1925), and appeared as the title character in *The Phantom of the Opera* that same year. The scene in which the Phantom is unmasked remains one of the truly fantastic and shocking scenes in the whole history of cinema. He continued to develop his transformative art form, working with Browning again in *The Blackbird* (1926), playing a man who pretends to be two brothers, *The Road to Mandalay* (1926), as a one-eyed crook, and *The Unknown* (1927) as Alonzo the Armless. He was a vampire in Browning's notorious *London After Midnight* (1927). Chaney's first talkie was a remake of his own *The Unholy Three* (1930).

Bizarrely, for someone who'd made his name as a silent star, Chaney's life was ended by cancer of the throat. He died in 1930, aged only 44 and having made over 140 movies. He'd been scheduled to join Tod Browning once again to play the title role in his version of *Dracula* (1933). The role went to Bela Lugosi, but the thought of Chaney as the Transylvanian Count is an intriguing one. Chaney's son, Lon Chaney Jr, would go on to realise another of Universal's archetypal movie monsters: the Wolfman.

Contemporary Equivalent: Ron Perlman (for his career as movie monsters, from the Beast to Hellboy) or Jim Carrey who achieves the same effect through facial contortions.

JOHN GILBERT (1895-1936)

John Gilbert, born John Pringle in Utah, was the archetypal silent era star whose career was ended with the coming of sound. The story goes that his handsome good looks were not complemented by his less-than-handsome voice. Conspiracy theories would have it that Gilbert's studio, MGM, tired of his salary demands and 'difficult' behaviour, failed to help the star adjust to the world of cinematic sound, as they had so many others, willing him to fail.

Gilbert was the modern cliché of a silent movie actor: demonstrative, often posing and posturing, rather than acting as we understand it today. He was an obvious and heavy-handed actor, and the coming of sound did not help him extend his career. Studio publicity had dubbed Gilbert 'the great lover', a role he then decided to try and emulate in real-life off screen. Teamed up with Greta Garbo by MGM, the pair fell in love off camera. Using their relationship as the centrepiece of Gilbert's publicity, MGM effectively killed the romance. A studio-sanctioned wedding collapsed in 1926 when Garbo left Gilbert standing impotently at the altar.

Gilbert's entry into movies dated back to cinema's earliest days, playing parts for Thomas H. Ince. He became more prominent in the early 1920s, working at Fox. Although in steady employment, Gilbert lacked a decisive role with which he became identified. He drifted from film to film, before making more of an impact at MGM in the mid-1920s in films such as *The Big Parade* (1925), *The Merry Widow* (1925) and opposite Garbo in *Flesh and the Devil* (1926). Of the pairing, Garbo came out on top.

As the silent era came to an end, Gilbert selected what he thought was a safe role for his sound debut, as Romeo to Norma Shearer's Juliet in a cameo sequence from *Hollywood Revue of 1929* (1929). His sound films failed, one after another, resulting in Gilbert taking out a self-financed advert in *Variety* claiming that MGM would neither offer him decent roles nor release him from his contract. Still stung by MGM's interference and manipulation of his relationship with Garbo, Gilbert was sinking, but he'd attempt to inflict some damage on the studio that'd brought him down.

Garbo attempted to rescue her former lover by requesting him as her co-star in 1933's *Queen Christina*, but it was not enough. His last film was made in 1935, and he was dead of alcoholism a year later, having been married four times and had Greta Garbo and (possibly) Marlene Dietrich as mistresses.

Contemporary Equivalent: The overrated everyman Tom Hanks.

CLARA BOW (1905-1965)

Clara Bow was the 'It' girl of America in the 1920s, the iconic image of the 'flapper', sexually aware and sexually available. She captured, represented and fulfilled all the promise of that fast-moving decade, the machine-age, when women were liberated and free to go after what they wanted. As one of the cinema's earliest 'sex symbols', Bow was exploited as much as she exploited the system to her own advantage. Her image became one of mass-marketed sexuality – a proto-Marilyn Monroe.

She was an ex-Beauty queen – a sure-fire path into movies then and now – and she started in the movies in low-key bit parts, watching and waiting for the main chance. She was among the first breed of movie actresses who knew how to play to the camera, to seduce the viewer, as if in a one-to-one relationship, not the one-to-many that was the communal experience of cinema. Her appeal was strongest in the mid-1920s, in films such as *Grit* (1924), *Wine* (1924), *Helen's Babies* (1925), *Eve's Lover* (1925) and *Kiss Me Again* (1925), directed by Mary Pickford's import, Ernst Lubitsch.

Following a move to Paramount, along with B.P. Schulberg, the director who 'discovered' her, Bow's prospects improved again. In 1927, she was shopgirl Betty Lou who seduces her boss in *It* (1927), the film that gave rise to the phrase 'the It girl', the 'It' in question being, simply and straightforwardly, sex. A huge star, Bow even appeared in a colour sequence in 1928's *Red Hair*, ideal to display her own dramatic hair colour and her lipstick coated pursed lips. By 1930, and the coming of sound, Bow was only 25 but had made almost 50 movies... Sound, however,

Clara Bow, *Wings* (1927)

revealed that the darling of the movies spoke with a rough-and-ready Brooklyn accent, the place she'd been born early in the century, and cramped her freewheeling style somewhat, as the clunky sound equipment meant more static cameras and settings. Caught up in sex scandals and gambling debts, Bow spent the 1930s in the newspapers more often than she was seen in cinemas. She continued to make films until the mid-1930s, before retiring from the screen as her weight ballooned and her reputation shrank.

Contemporary Equivalent: Paris Hilton.

THE SILENT CLOWNS

Of all the silent stars, it's the comedians who were the most popular and who still live on today. When people think of silent cinema, it is often the image of Charlie Chaplin's little tramp, or a Mack Sennett Keystone Kops chase that comes to mind. The most widely available of silent cinema, and most widely appreciated, the comedy films have been seen on TV from the 1960s through to the late 1980s and formed a large part of the video and DVD market, appealing to enthusiasts, film buffs and general audiences alike. After all, there's a reason that Charlie Chaplin remains the biggest worldwide movie star of all time...

CHARLIE CHAPLIN (1889-1977)

Love him or loathe him, Charlie Chaplin's 'little tramp' character is many people's only perception of silent cinema. The reason he's still a prime figure in cinema, silent or otherwise, 30 years after his death is due to the impact he had in the years between his debut in 1914 and his final film in 1967, one of the industry's longest careers. While many of silent cinema's pioneers took control of their own careers, no one managed it to quite the extent that Chaplin did. He began as a mere actor, a clown, attracted to the new medium in its earliest days.

From extreme poverty in the East End of London to the music hall stage, Chaplin joined Fred Karno's vaudeville company alongside another young performer, Stan Laurel. During 1908, Chaplin became a regular, featuring in many of Karno's performances, playing a whole variety of exaggerated characters. Countless of Chaplin's earliest films would find their inspiration in the simple scenarios presented by Fred Karno. By 1910, Chaplin and Laurel were part of the Karno troupe touring America. Chaplin loudly declared it was his intention to conquer the continent. There's a 1911 photograph of the Karno performers which sees Chaplin sporting a fake moustache much like that of his later film character, a good three years before the 'little tramp' character made his debut.

A second tour of the US in 1913 saw Chaplin, whose fame was increasing, hired by Mack Sennett's Keystone studios. As a company, Keystone was only two years old. Best known, prior to Chaplin's arrival, for the Keystone Kops and Fatty Arbuckle, Keystone had contacted Karno with a cable requesting contact with 'Chaffin, in your company, or something like that...' It was close enough to get to Chaplin. He was hired to make movies at $150 per week, doubling his Karno earnings. He was 24 years old and figured that a year doing movies would increase his profile enough that he could return to vaudeville at the top of the bill.

Chaplin had a steep learning curve in cinema, and soon grasped the principles of shooting on location, out of sequence and the basics of editing. Quickly enough, he rose to the challenges and wanted to push cinema even further. This led to clashes with his first directors, including Henry Lehrman, for even this early in the industry's development production techniques were becoming established and fixed in place. Chaplin – as a newcomer to the business – was able to bring a fresh sense of experimentation to his work. He sported a monocle and a long moustache in his film debut *Making a Living* (1914), and it was in his second, *Kid Auto Races at Venice* (1914) – shot on location during a real event – that Chaplin's tramp costume and persona appeared on screen for the first time. His third film, *Mabel's Strange Predicament* (1914), saw Chaplin steal the film from his more established co-star Mabel Normand. As much as Chaplin learned about the basics of making films from the people at Keystone, they also learnt from his years of stagecraft in vaudeville, bringing a new, largely English, source of material to the conveyer belt production line that was early cinema.

CHARLIE CHAPLIN
(CHARLOT)

125

Charlie Chaplin

Chaplin quickly became a huge international star having featured in 35 successful shorts (the lack of sound lending him appeal across language barriers), resulting in his demanding a salary increase to $1,000 per week, more than even Sennett was earning. Refused by Sennett, Chaplin's requirements were met by Essanay, so he started at the new studio in 1915. Founded in 1907 by George K. Spoor and G.M. 'Broncho Billy' Anderson (the S and A of the name), Essanay's stars were their Broncho Billy Westerns and cross-eyed comedian Ben Turpin. Full page ads in January 1916 editions of *Motion Picture News* and *Moving Picture World*, placed by Essanay, declared Chaplin to be the world's 'greatest, funniest' comedian.

Chaplin arrived at Essanay's Chicago studios from California, expecting a greater degree of creative autonomy than he'd enjoyed at Keystone. He discovered instead that scripts were allocated to performers on a seemingly ad hoc basis, regardless of suitability. Chaplin also disliked the climate, so only made one film – *His New Job* (1915) – in Chicago, before relocating back to Essanay's Californian production facility in San Francisco, where distance from his new bosses allowed him the creative independence he craved.

By April that year Chaplin was back in Los Angeles, where he'd started, running his own production unit. Such was the little clown's fame that when shooting on location around Los Angeles it was sometimes necessary to erect barriers to keep fans and the curious away from the filming. The level of secrecy surrounding Chaplin and his working methods had never been seen before in Hollywood. It seems this was inspired by the need to shield Chaplin from studios keen to poach his talents, as Essanay had, as much as to create a sense of mystique around the little tramp. Chaplin was often short-tempered when making movies, taking out his frustrations on his co-stars. As a perfectionist, he would drive them crazy by shooting repeated takes of scenes until he was entirely happy with the result. This shooting and re-shooting only came after many, many days of rehearsal. The result of this obsessive approach to his creative work was a series of films that still speak to audiences today.

It's difficult now, looking back, to comprehend the sheer scale of Chaplin's fame. *Pictures and the Picturegoer* claimed, on 18 September 1915, 'There is no one more talked about than the inimitable Charlie Chaplin. In fact, the world is Chaplin mad!'[8] The figure of the little tramp was known and laughed at around the world, regardless of language. No movie star has been as big or had such wide appeal since the coming of sound. Chaplin became the subject of much press and the target of all sorts of speculation as to his background, his personal life and his plans for the future. The demand for film prints featuring Chaplin was so great that a huge business trafficking in illegal pirate copies grew, distributing Chaplin's image even further afield. There was official Chaplin merchandise, but the vast majority of material produced was unlicensed, including Chaplin dolls, fan magazines, comic strips featuring the little tramp, songs and musicals, even impersonators, costumes to buy and animated cartoons. *Tatler* published a cover portrait of Chaplin out of his little tramp gear on 15 March 1916, dubbing him 'possibly the widest known personage in the world'.[9]

Increasingly unhappy at Essanay, Chaplin had been offered $350,000 for a further 12 two-reel films. Now managed by his brother Syd, Chaplin demanded an additional $150,000 bonus from Essanay, which was refused. Syd began negotiations with rival film company Mutual, only for Chaplin – who increasingly feared the bubble of his popularity was about to burst – to demand an advance of $100,000 up front. Mutual had previously distributed the old Keystone Chaplin films and was keen to sign the star for a new series of pictures. Chaplin's financial demands were hard to meet, however. Nonetheless, on 26 February 1916, Chaplin signed a new contract with Mutual. Chaplin was to be paid $10,000 per week, plus a signing bonus of $150,000, an unprecedented amount of money in Hollywood. Chaplin claimed that he was uninterested in the money, because it got in the way of his comic creativity, simply leaving the details to Syd and Mutual.

Chaplin brought Edna Purviance to Mutual with him to continue as his leading lady (and real-life romantic partner), while other Essanay colleagues also featured in the Mutual films. Although contracted to produce 12 films over one year, Chaplin took 17 months to fulfil his contract due to delays caused by the building of his own studio facilities and illness. For Chaplin, the Mutual period was the happiest of his creative life and it certainly produced the best and most well-remembered of his short films, including *The Floorwalker*, *The Vagabond*, *The Rink*, *Easy Street*, *The Cure* and *The Immigrant*.

Mutual tried to retain Chaplin, but were out-bid by First National in 1917. Again, the cost of being in business with Chaplin increased, to around $1 million for 12 short films, plus another $75,000 signing bonus. Chaplin had complete control over his productions and was able to, once again, build an entirely new production facility at La Brea Avenue in Los Angeles. He continued to use the same studio space until his final departure from the US. For his part of the deal, Chaplin had to deliver eight two-reel films within sixteen months with a per film budget of $125,000. Chaplin's Mutual sparring partner, the larger than life Eric Campbell died before the star's switch to First National, but Edna Purviance was along for the ride, as well as Chaplin's trusted brother Syd.

Chaplin's involvement with First National limited his participation in United Artists, the studio he set up with Mary Pickford, Douglas Fairbanks and DW Griffith in 1919. Chaplin had slowed his work rate by this time, spending more time experimenting with cinematic form. First National refused to release his documentary project *How To Make Movies* and expressed worries about their star's idiosyncratic work methods. It took Chaplin five years to complete what had been intended as a sixteen-month contract. After the successful double whammy of *A Dog's Life* (1918) and *Shoulder Arms* (1918), both regarded as classic films, Chaplin seemed to lose inspiration or enthusiasm, or both. Additionally, the press who'd done so much to build Chaplin turned on the world's most popular comedian, declaring *Sunnyside* (1918) to be the beginning of the end for the little tramp. According to *Theater Magazine*, Chaplin would fall into obscurity within five years.

The troubled making of *The Kid* (1921), Chaplin's first feature length movie, alarmed First National even further. Chaplin attempted to buy himself out of the contract, but the studio refused, despite their worries – after all, better they had Chaplin under contract, whatever the problems, than their competitors should benefit from his comic genius. Chaplin's final three short films, *The Idle Class* (1921), *Pay Day* (1922) and *The Pilgrim* (1923), completed his First National commitment.

Free of First National, Chaplin's debut film for United Artists wasn't a comedy at all but the drama *A Woman of Paris* (1923), which starred Edna Purviance. Although publicly Chaplin claimed he didn't appear in the film at all, he did disguise himself as a porter for a cameo. *The Gold Rush* (1925) followed, and remains an iconic film today. Chaplin's last release before the coming of sound was *The Circus* (1928). The film was made at a time of personal difficulty (a camera fault scratched the negatives of the first month's work, there was a fire at his studio which destroyed a stage, he had serious tax problems and was getting divorced from actress Lita Grey), yet it won him an Oscar in the first year the Academy Awards were presented.

Like every other silent film artist, Chaplin faced the coming of sound with some trepidation. Some, like Laurel and Hardy, benefited enormously from sound, while others, like Harold Lloyd and Buster Keaton fared less well. Chaplin began making *City Lights* in 1928, well aware that his industry was moving to adopt sound. He simply refused to change his techniques, eschewing recorded synchronised sound, opting instead for a musical score and occasional sound effects. So prolonged were his working methods that *City Lights* wasn't released until 1931, a seemingly anachronistic film among all the sound movies. However, the film was a hit. Chaplin claimed silent film to be a separate art form, one within which it was legitimate to continue working, while those around him leapt upon the new sound technology.

For many, Chaplin's refusal to move with the times was initially welcome. *Modern Times* (1936) continued his exploration of the art of silent cinema, introducing occasional voices and climaxing with the 'little tramp' character 'speaking' by singing a nonsense song. Finally, a decade after everyone else, Charlie Chaplin embarked upon a series of talkies: *The Great Dictator* (1940), *Monsieur Verdoux* (1947), *Limelight* (1952) – exploring his own past in vaudeville and featuring Buster Keaton – and *A King in New York* (1957). His final film was *A Countess of Hong Kong* (1967), which he wrote and directed, but only appeared in via a brief cameo as a steward. By this time, Chaplin's controversial left-wing politics (and history of sex scandals) had seen him exiled from the USA to Europe.

Chaplin was, of course, more than just a cinema clown: his films exhibited a degree of poetry and pathos among the humour that few others could achieve or even aspire to. His work has been in and out of favour in the 30 years since his death in 1977, but he is considered prime among the top three cinematic clowns of the silent era, the others being Buster Keaton and Harold Lloyd.

BUSTER KEATON (1895-1966)

For a long time cultural critics championed 'the Great Stone Face', as Buster Keaton was widely known, as 'better than Chaplin'. It took a while, but from his death in the mid-1960s through to the age of DVD, Keaton has finally been canonised as one of the three classic silent clowns, alongside Chaplin and Lloyd.

Joseph Frank Keaton, born into a family of Vaudevillians in 1895, gained the nickname 'Buster' from none other than the great escapologist Harry Houdini. From the time he could work, Keaton was part of his parents' – Joe and Mary's – touring act, learning the immediate basics of pratfalls and stage acrobatics. His athletic clowning came through in many of his films, but that was far from all that Keaton achieved.

When the family act wound down in 1917, Keaton found his way to Joseph Schenck's New York film production studio and was quickly teamed up with Roscoe 'Fatty' Arbuckle in the 'Comique' series of films. Arbuckle started in 1909 and was one of the few actors whose name

Buster Keaton, *The Goat* (1921)

formed part of his movies' titles. He was a regular at Keystone when Chaplin arrived in 1913, so by the time Keaton joined at Schenck's studio, he was teaming with a successful and famous star. By 1918, the studio and its two lead actors had relocated to California, along with the rest of the emerging 'Hollywood' movie industry.

Keaton was interested in the behind-the-scenes process of filmmaking. He quickly learned every technique he could, co-directing many of the Arbuckle/Keaton comedy shorts without formal credit. During early productions like *The Butcher Boy* (Keaton's debut, 1917), *Fatty at Coney Island* (1917), *Oh, Doctor!* (1917) and *The Bell Boy* (1918), Keaton would laugh and smile like the rest of the performers, but he soon came to realise that he won a stronger reaction from audiences by keeping a straight face when responding to comic situations. Thus was born 'the Great Stone Face'.

By 1920, Keaton had moved on from Arbuckle, starred in a series of 19 solo shorts and begun making comic feature films with *The Saphead* (1920). In this work, Keaton had total autonomy and creative control. Many themes emerge, but one repeated in his short films is 'man versus machine', with the mechanical age personified in the shape of recalcitrant houses. In *One Week* (1920), Keaton and co-star Sybil Sealy set up home in a cheap kit-house, which Keaton has to build himself. The resulting lop-sided home is later demolished by a train. *The Haunted House* (1921) and *The Electric House* (1922) both see mechanical devices (operated by crooks in *The Haunted House*) providing a great deal of comic business for Keaton. Keaton actually broke his leg on the mechanical staircase in *The Electric House*.

Relationships were also central to Keaton's comedy, even when those in his private life were no laughing matter. *The Boat* (1921) sees Keaton as a family man, whose sons are his spitting image. In *Hard Luck* (1921), Keaton's dramatic high dive takes him through the Earth and back, with a new family in tow. *My Wife's Relations* (1921), a tale of an oppressive extended family, reflected Keaton's real-life troubles. Keaton had married Natalie Talmadge (Schenck's sister-in-law) in 1921, only to discover that her interfering sisters Norma and Constance seemed to be part of the package. Natalie and Keaton seemed like a fortuitous match, but unfortunately the pair had little in common and both were largely dependent on others: Keaton on whomever was around to look after him (at this stage Natalie, later – in his more financially successful times – his butler), and Natalie on her more successful and glamorous sisters. The pair quickly drifted apart, with Keaton embarking on a series of affairs and turning to drink for solace. Two children – James and Robert – resulted from the marriage by 1924, but by the end of that year, their relationship was little more than an 'in-name-only' arrangement. Keaton had never been good at dealing with business or handling his money and had signed over the income from his company, Buster Keaton Productions, to Natalie in 1922.

On screen, Keaton's comic power was going from strength-to-strength, despite his problems at home and increasing reliance on alcohol. A series of classic films began with his spoof of Griffith's *Intolerance*, *Three Ages* (1923), which saw Keaton portray three different men with relationship troubles in three different time periods: pre-history, Roman, and the then-present of the 1920s. *Our Hospitality* (1923) followed, as did *Sherlock Jr* (1924), a bonafide cinema classic that sees Keaton play a film projectionist who dreams himself into the movie he's screening. Critic David Thompson called *Sherlock Jr* 'the most philosophically eloquent of silent comedies. Only an artist aware of the complex appeal to fantasy in cinema could have conceived it.'[10]

The Navigator (1924), *Go West* (1925), *Seven Chances* (1925) and *Battling Butler* (1926) led to Keaton's cinematic masterpiece, *The General* (1927). An American Civil War-set comedy, *The General* is an epic, cinematic tour-de-force that stands the test of time today. Full of fantastic business on and around the steam train of the title, *The General* features an epic recreation of the action of the Civil War as a picturesque backdrop to Keaton's comic activities. Although not a great success upon first release in 1927, *The General* has gone on to be regarded as Keaton's best film.

The General was the high point of Keaton's filmmaking career, a pinnacle he'd never reach again. *College* (1927) and *Steamboat Bill Jr* (1928) almost saw him through to the end of the silent era. Keaton signed a new deal at MGM, where he became a comic-for-hire, and lost his autonomy and creative control. From *The Cameraman* (1928) onwards, Keaton's own input was lessened, via *Spite Marriage* (1929) and Keaton's first 'talkie', *Free and Easy* (1930), to *Doughboys* (1930). All made money, but the quality was decreasing and the Depression was biting hard, as the novelty of 'talkies' wore off. A pairing with wisecracking comic Jimmy Durante was the end of Keaton's mainstream film career. By 1933, he was out of work, his marriage was over and his alcoholism was worsening. He made movies in France and the UK, but the 1930s were something of a creative wasteland for 'the Great Stone Face'. A brief second marriage and increasing medical problems didn't help. He resorted to making short films for Educational Studios (between 1934 and 1947) and at Columbia (1939-41), and by 1940 was into his third marriage. Occasional film appearances followed, but it wasn't until the 1950s and roles in *Sunset Boulevard* (1950) and Charlie Chaplin's ode to vaudeville, *Limelight* (1953), that Keaton appeared in anything significant.

It was television in the mid-1950s and the 1960s that brought Keaton's art to life once more, through screenings of his earlier films, documentaries about his career and frequent guest appearances, driven by Keaton's need for an income. One of his best TV appearances was in a 1961 episode of *The Twilight Zone* called 'Once Upon a Time'. Keaton gets to reprise much of his trademark slapstick material as an inventor transported from 1890 to 1962. It's a lovely homage to silent movies.

Keaton lived to see the reappraisal of his career in the 1960s, especially a new appreciation for *The General*, which led to him featuring in a 25-minute follow-up, *The Railrodder* (1965), and an influential documentary, *Buster Keaton Rides Again* (1965). His final film was Richard Lester's *A Funny Thing Happened on the Way to the Forum* (1966). Working until the end, Keaton died aged 70, having basked in his newfound critical approval and the reappraisal of *The General*.

HAROLD LLOYD (1893-1971)

Accorded 'third genius' status after Chaplin and Keaton, Harold Lloyd ironically out-grossed both during the 1920s, as the most popular silent screen comedian. Known today as a king of 'daredevil comedy', thanks to the iconic image of Lloyd's 'glasses' character hanging from the hands of a clock near the top of a skyscraper, Lloyd was anything but. His appealing character was a go-getting, optimistic insider in society, a contrast to the outsiders played by Chaplin and Keaton.

Lloyd had an itinerant childhood in Nebraska, due to his father 'Foxy' Lloyd's various failed attempts to get on in the world. Early stage experience quickly led Lloyd to California where he featured as an extra in

Harold Lloyd

The Old Monk's Tale, an early Edison film from 1913. Learning the film business, Lloyd hooked up with fellow actor Hal Roach (later producer of Laurel & Hardy's best work) in 1915. He began with an uninspired pair of Chaplin knock-off characters: Willie Work (in six single-reel movies) and Lonesome Luke (wearing tight clothes, instead of baggy – like

Chaplin – but sporting the same hat-and-cane combo). In between, Lloyd briefly worked at Mack Sennett's Keystone studio, appearing with Fatty Arbuckle in *Miss Fatty's Seaside Lovers* (1916). The Luke comedies ran until 1917, developing into two reelers. Very few survive today, with the negatives destroyed in a film vault fire in 1943. It was late in 1917 when Lloyd finally adopted the 'glasses' character that would make his name. One of the surviving Luke comedies, *Luke's Movie Muddle* (1917), features a supporting character sporting large horn-rimmed round-framed glasses. It was from this – according to Roach – that Lloyd developed his own trademark look, escaping the shadow of Chaplin.

Over the Fence (1917) marked the debut of the 'new' Harold Lloyd. Hedging his bets, Roach insisted that Lloyd alternate the 'glasses' shorts with continued Luke films, which Lloyd agreed to do until it became clear that the 'glasses' character was a winner. The shadow of Chaplin was still evident in the style and gags of these early 'glasses' films, but as Lloyd and Roach became more confident, Lloyd found himself developing a unique 'go-getter' who reflected the spirit of the times. Another factor that marked Lloyd as different from the other silent clowns was his willingness to employ sudden violence, especially in these earlier shorts.

The first sign of things to come featured in *Look Out Below* (1918), in which Lloyd uses one of the newly rising skyscrapers as the basis of an early 'thrill' comedy. Although these climbing capers constitute a fraction of his output, they provided Lloyd's iconic image. As he would later do in his best-known 'climbing film', *Safety Last* (1923), Lloyd used a safety platform to create the illusion he was hanging from the edge of a skyscraper with nothing between him and the ground. He moved into two-reelers featuring the 'glasses' character in 1919, starting with *Bumping into Broadway* (1919).

Throughout the one-reelers, Lloyd had built up a small rep company of actors, primarily comprising actress Bebe Daniels (aged only 15 when she started) and Snub Pollard. Lloyd also dated Daniels for much of their time working together, but she quit both Lloyd's films and his life when she left to pursue a drama career with Cecil B. DeMille. Lloyd replaced

Daniels with Mildred Davis, who went on to become his wife (until her death in 1969, two years before Lloyd's) as well as his co-star for the remainder of his shorts and into his early feature films, quitting after *Safety Last*.

In 1919, during shooting for *Haunted Spooks*, Lloyd was required to take part in a stills photography session to create some promotional images. Posing with what he believed was a prop bomb and pretending to use the lit fuse to light a cigarette, Lloyd was stunned when the 'dummy' bomb exploded in his hand. While seriously injured – losing his thumb and forefinger, and temporarily blinded – Lloyd was lucky that he was holding the bomb away from his face and head when it exploded, blowing a hole in the studio roof instead of in his head. Lloyd never talked about losing part of his hand, and in his films and public appearances until the end of his life he used a series of prosthetic gloves to replace the missing thumb and finger. This makes his later 'daredevil' comedy films and climbing stunts all the more remarkable.

It was 1920 before Lloyd returned to the screen in *An Eastern Westerner*. More high jinks followed in the ledge walking scenes of *High and Dizzy* (1920), proving that Lloyd had lost none of his cinematic daring. Lloyd's films grew in length from two to three and four reelers. He worked instinctively, dreaming up a series of scenarios with his gag writers then shooting the films in sections and only slotting them together at the end, hence the variable lengths. *I Do* (1921) Lloyd's final two-reeler, with *Never Weaken* (1921), which sees him blindfolded, and hoisted through the air and across a skyscraper under construction on a girder, was his final three-reeler. Lloyd's first feature is generally considered to be *A Sailor Made Man* (1921), at four-reels just about an hour in length. His official first feature was the five-reel *Grandma's Boy* (1922), which began as a short but grew in the making.

More features rapidly followed: *Dr Jack* (1922), the classic *Safety Last* (1923) – in typical Lloyd style, he shot the building climbing climax first with no idea of how the story would lead to that – then *Why Worry?* (1923), Lloyd's final film for Roach, which introduced new leading lady,

Jobyna Ralston. By now, Harold Lloyd's films were extremely popular, and Lloyd himself was able to command 80 per cent of the film's profits. Following the split from Roach, Lloyd established the Harold Lloyd Corporation to handle the production of his movies and he wisely bought up control of his entire back catalogue. *Girl Shy* (1924) was the first feature produced by the newly independent Lloyd. Playing a shy tailor, Harold Meadows, Lloyd's character has learned enough about women to write a 'how to' book on seduction. On a train journey he meets Mary (Ralston), with whom he strikes up a friendship despite his shyness. Realising she is about to marry a bigamist, he leaps into action in an attempt to stop the ceremony and save Mary. Much comic complication follows as Harold uses trains, a series of cars and, eventually, a horse and a fire engine to get to the church on time.

More films cemented Harold Lloyd's popularity and drew bigger box office grosses than either Chaplin or Keaton. Another wedding leads to matrimonial comedy in *Hot Water* (1924), while *The Freshman* (1925) sees him play a college student who likes to be called 'Speedy' – Lloyd's real-life nickname and the title of a later film. The climatic football game of *The Freshman* was reprised in *The Sin of Harold Diddlebock* (aka *Mad Wednesday*, 1947), Lloyd's comeback movie after a decade away from the screen, with Preston Sturges directing.

Lloyd switched his distribution from a long-running deal with Pathé to Paramount for *For Heaven's Sake* (1926), his first flop. *The Kid Brother* (1927) and *Speedy* (1928), both action-adventure comedies followed, the latter notable for its dramatic location shooting in New York. *Welcome Danger* (1929) began life as another silent film, but Lloyd quickly realised that the coming of sound would change the film business entirely, although he didn't much like it personally. *Welcome Danger* was converted mid-production to a sound film, which involved much expensive re-shooting, pushing the film over budget. The first film Lloyd made as a talkie was *Feet First* (1930), but he didn't seem to strike the same chord with audiences as a talking clown as he had as a silent character. From here until his withdrawal from movies, Lloyd experienced a series of diminishing returns as the films became more expensive and the box office returns decreased.

Sound brought in a new, younger breed of verbal clowns, so the likes of *Movie Crazy* (1932), *The Cat's Paw* (1934), *The Milky Way* (1936) and *Professor Beware* (1938) were not hits. Lloyd retired from films, taking up 3D photography in his Greenacres estate, a mansion built on a huge tract of land bought with his movie profits. He received a special Oscar in 1952 and was featured on the US *This is Your Life* show in 1955. Owning the rights to his own films and never happy with the way TV treated old movies, he kept his own off television through the 1950s and 1960s. As a result, a couple of generations grew up with Chaplin but remained unaware of Harold Lloyd.

In the 1960s, he constructed and released two compilation films: *Harold Lloyd's World of Comedy* (1962) and *Harold Lloyd's Funny Side of Life* (1966) to great acclaim. These movies fed into the rediscovery of silent film in the 1960s, and Lloyd was soon added to the list of top practitioners of the art alongside Chaplin and Keaton. He died in 1971 having worked with some young fans of his work to sort out the film material held in his vaults, thus making the later re-release of his films (now available on DVD) possible.

ROSCOE 'FATTY' ARBUCKLE (1887-1933)

See Chapter 8: Silent Scandals

THE OTHER SILENT CLOWNS

The other minor screen clowns remembered by aficionados of silent comedy have failed to make the crossover to the popular imagination in the way Chaplin, Lloyd and Keaton did. Their work is rarely screened on television, though some is available on DVD, bringing a whole new audience to these other practitioners of silent screen comedy beyond the big three and the scandal-ridden Arbuckle.

Ben Turpin (1874-1940) is recalled largely due to his cross-eyed appearance. He spent over a decade on the vaudeville stage before coming to the screen via Essanay studios in 1907. Jumping between stage and screen, Turpin's earliest success came as a sidekick to Charlie Chaplin in the shorts *His New Job* (1915) and *A Night Out* (1915). Failing to adapt to Chaplin's meticulous approach, Turpin soon moved on to work for Mack Sennett and appeared in a lengthy series of comedies opposite Heinie Conklin (aka Charlie Lynn). By the 1920s, Turpin was featuring in Sennett films such as *A Small Town Idol* (1921) and *Yukon Jake* (1924). Physical gags and his unique looks saw Turpin through the 1920s, followed by a dignified retirement from films with occasional appearances in a WC Fields film (*Million Dollar Legs*) and a couple of Laurel & Hardy talkies (*Our Wife*, *Saps at Sea*). He died in 1940.

Harry Langdon (1884-1944) was a strange, baby-faced combination of Charlie Chaplin and Harold Lloyd. Another vaudeville veteran, Langdon was a Sennett screen comedian in the early 1920s, whose career was built on a trademark vaudeville sketch about a collapsing limo called 'Johnny's New Car'. Langdon was not a neat fit at Sennett, however. Although verging on 40 when he came to prominence, Langdon's white face make-up gave him a child-like appearance (shades of Mary Pickford) and he was often cast as a Chaplin-like innocent. He wasn't up to the usual fast-paced slapstick Sennett fare, and he lacked the distinctive unusual looks of someone like Ben Turpin. He was placed in the normal Sennett farce-and-chase films, such as *Picking Peaches* (1924) and *Smile, Please* (1924). He later settled into the role of a slow-paced bumbler, where he would come good at the end without actually making any effort. Naïve and prone to coincidence, Langdon's characters would succeed in the world without really trying, and certainly not at the Sennett breakneck pace. Whatever job he takes on, he's somehow out-of-place or unprepared, such as the world's softest lumberjack in *Boobs in the Woods* (1925) or an inept soldier fighting the war long after it's finished in the three-reeler *Soldier Man* (1926). Langdon finished working for Sennett in 1926 after 23 shorts and a feature, *His First Flame* (released in 1927).

He then set-up his own company, and released his films through First National, several of which were written or co-written by Frank Capra (future director of classics like *It's A Wonderful Life*, 1946). His first film under his own production banner, *Tramp, Tramp, Tramp*, co-starred a very young Joan Crawford (*Mildred Pierce*). His second film, *The Strong Man* (1926), is often considered his best. Capra directed this tale of a World War I soldier who's handier with a catapult than a rifle. The slow-burn comedy and sense of Langdon being a protected idiot who can suffer no wrong is perfected here. The film was critically acclaimed by contemporary reviewers, sealing Langdon's reputation as a great second-string screen clown. Capra continued to direct Langdon in *Long Pants*, which included a Technicolor sequence, but their relationship dissolved when Capra branched out on his own. Langdon began directing his own films with *Three's A Crowd* (1928) and *The Chaser* (1928), but seemed to lose sight of what made his comedy work.

Langdon's last silent, *Heart Trouble* (1928), saw his reviews improve but seemed to confuse and disappoint his audience. The coming of sound killed Langdon's career, as with so many other silent stars. He worked with Hal Roach (who produced Laurel & Hardy and for whom Langdon would work as a gag writer late in his career), but his thin voice failed to match with the comedy character he was attached to. Minor shorts for Educational and Columbia followed, with a return to a co-starring role opposite Oliver Hardy in the latter's solo film *Zenobia* (1939). Capra and Sennett both suggested that Langdon's career failed when he attempted to direct himself. A skilled gagman and comedy writer, it does appear that Langdon needed the control and direction of others to shape his comedy.

Charley Chase (1893-1940) almost bypassed vaudeville altogether. Instead, he made a splash in films at Keystone after a brief period on stage. He appeared alongside Chaplin in *His New Profession* (1914) and *His*

Musical Career (1914), before becoming a director at Keystone and Fox. Working at Hal Roach's studios, Chase directed a series of Snub Pollard shorts, while also helming many of the Our Gang comedies. Chase used his real name of Charles Parrott when directing, often working in Hollywood's new studios alongside his director brother James Parrott. Chase was back on screen in 1924, starring in a series of one-reelers for Roach. Director Leo McCarey developed Chase's persona of frustrated ambition as the shorts expanded to two-reelers. There's something of Harold Lloyd (albeit taller and thinner) in Charley Chase. This similarity to a well-established screen comedian may have prevented Chase from becoming a top tier star. His regular appearances in lame marital farces probably didn't help. He made the move to Universal and feature films with *Modern Love* (1929), just as sound arrived. More shorts at Roach and Columbia followed, as well as directing gigs on shorts for The Three Stooges. He never fulfilled his potential, though mentored many other comedians behind the scenes. Personal problems and alcoholism contributed to his early death in 1940 from a heart attack.

SILENT SCANDALS

The establishment of the basics of cinema was a rapid affair. Within a few years after the invention of moving pictures, the novelty of capturing and projecting reality had been surpassed by structured narratives, which were helmed by directors and featured recognisable stars. The public, despite their awareness of directors like Cecil B. DeMille who represented a particular style of film, were more involved with the personalities on the screen: the stars. The growing Hollywood colony allowed the new, often exceedingly well-paid stars to indulge their excesses. A host of Hollywood star scandals in the late teens and early 1920s drew attention to the morals of the movie world, attracting censorship both from outside and within the movie industry. Hollywood quickly realised it had an image problem, one that had to be addressed by controlling the on-screen talent's off-screen activities.

From the accusation of raping and murdering a young actress made against comedian Fatty Arbuckle in 1921 to the still unsolved murder of director William Desmond Taylor, and the scandalous divorce of 'America's sweetheart' actress Mary Pickford from matinee idol Douglas Fairbanks, the spotlight was on Hollywood.

The solution, as far as the studios were concerned, was Will Hays, hired to boost the film industry's declining reputation by reassuring the nation that Hollywood was not a hotbed of scandal. As a result of the stars who fell from movie heaven, the movie industry would now censor itself. The resulting 'Production Code' was the first in Hollywood to list specific restrictions on language and behaviour, particularly sex and crime, ironically the two most basic sure-fire box office draws. Nudity, dancing, religion, illegal drug use, venereal disease, childbirth and miscegenation would all come under the 'Hays' Code'. Although the Production Code was enacted in 1930 and had a major impact on the first flowering of sound cinema, it was the scandals of the silent era that created the conditions that made the code necessary to protect the newly formed film industry.

ROSCOE 'FATTY' ARBUCKLE (1887-1933)

One of the most unjustly tragic downfalls in Hollywood history was that of Roscoe 'Fatty' Arbuckle, who went from lauded star name to industry pariah and death over the course of a decade and a half. Born in Kansas in 1887, Arbuckle moved to California as a child and found his way into movies in 1909, playing upon his physical bulk. He became known to the public as 'Fatty' Arbuckle, although he hated the nickname and the fact that he was famous as 'the fat screen comedian'. His earliest film work was undertaken while Arbuckle and his wife Minta Durfee toured the vaudeville circuit. By 1913, he was one of the prominent figures in the Keystone comedies. Although physically large, Arbuckle's dexterity and agility gave him a unique and distinctive screen presence, and he especially stood out among the Keystone Kops.

Arbuckle was soon headlining his own film series, with his nickname 'Fatty' often appearing in the titles, such as in *Fatty's Magic Pants* (1914) and *Fatty's Faithful Fido* (1915). Arbuckle quickly took creative control of his own films, directing many. He worked with Chaplin during his first days at Keystone, and one legend even suggests that it was Arbuckle who gave Chaplin the clothes that became the Little Tramp's identifying look. The pair made a handful of shorts together before Chaplin's departure for greater things and Arbuckle took up with Joseph Schenck and Buster Keaton (see Chapter 7: The Silent Clowns for more on Chaplin and Keaton).

Roscoe 'Fatty' Arbuckle

After the Keaton shorts, Arbuckle starred in seven feature films before the events of September 1921 brought his career crashing down. A raucous show business party on Labor Day in a San Francisco hotel ended with the suspicious death of starlet Virginia Rappé. Arbuckle was quickly accused of attacking or assaulting her and inflicting internal injuries that resulted in her death. The comedian was charged with manslaughter even though there was little or no evidence to support the widely circulated allegations. Coverage of the ensuing trials, led by the William Randolph Heart-owned newspapers, was heavily biased against Arbuckle and Hollywood. Henry Lehrman, one of Arbuckle's earliest directors who had been romantically involved with Rappé, was a particularly prominent critic. Others, such as Chaplin, came to Arbuckle's defence but were not given the same space in newspapers. After years of success, Arbuckle was targeted to take the fall for the whole of Hollywood.

The impression of a foregone conclusion in terms of Arbuckle's guilt was effectively created, especially as the process involved three separate trials, suggesting there was a determination on the part of the State to accept nothing but a guilty verdict. Yet a surprise verdict from the third and final jury saw Arbuckle acquitted in March 1922, and offered an unprecedented and profound apology by the jury.

The damage, however, was done. Arbuckle's last film, *Crazy to Marry* (1921), was pulled from cinemas, and two other completed films were not even released. His studio contract was cancelled and an all-encompassing, though unofficial, ban was placed upon the actor, even though he'd been declared not guilty. Roscoe 'Fatty' Arbuckle had gone from being a top comedy star for over seven years to unemployed, a signifier for everything that was morally wrong with Hollywood.

Buster Keaton supported Arbuckle after his fall from grace, even suggesting that he return as a director under the punning (and contrite) pseudonym of Will B. Goode. Arbuckle, in fact, achieved this using the name William Goodrich. He worked as a director at Educational Films and at RKO/Pathé until 1932, including the feature film *The Red Mill* (1927), starring Marion Davies, infamous now as the mistress of Arbuckle's nemesis William Randolph Hearst. The late-1920s saw a campaign among entertainers to rehabilitate Arbuckle in the public's estimation, resulting in his return to vaudeville and the screening of some of his films, in contravention of the Hays' Code. By 1931, movie magazine *Photoplay* had run a sympathetic article and interview with Arbuckle, in which he seemed resigned to his fate. Even so, he was back in front of the cameras for a brief series of sound shorts for Warner Bros./Vitaphone in 1932-33, following an industry petition calling for him to be allowed to work once more. It was too little, too late for Roscoe 'Fatty' Arbuckle, as he died of a heart attack in 1933, the same day that Warner Bros. offered the newly rising star a brand new feature film contract. It was a sad end to a short, creative life in which Arbuckle had suffered much injustice, and was largely remembered in the public imagination – wrongly – as the fat silent comedian who murdered an actress in one of the biggest Hollywood scandals of the 1920s.

WILLIAM DESMOND TAYLOR (1872-1922)

Fatty Arbuckle's frequent co-star Mabel Normand was the last person to see film director William Desmond Taylor alive. Taylor was at the heart of the growing movie business in Hollywood, having directed over 40 films since 1914. He was President of the Motion Pictures Directors' Association and had spent a great deal of time defending the morals of the movie colony as Arbuckle faced the first of his three trials. The 49-year-old Englishman was found during the night of 1 February 1922, shot in the back. Taylor's mysterious death was just the beginning of a long-running scandal that would rock the newly laid foundations of Hollywood.

Mabel Normand was one of the silent era's biggest comedy stars, known as much for her on and off romance with Keystone founder Mack Sennett as for her screen persona. Normand claimed she'd been collecting a couple of books from Taylor. In their brief meeting, Normand claimed Taylor had accused Edward F. Sands, his then missing secretary, of forging his cheques. Taylor had walked Normand to her car. That same evening Taylor had bailed his butler Henry Peavey from jail, where he was being held after an arrest for soliciting boys in a local park.

The following morning, Normand was phoned by fellow Hollywood comedy star, and Chaplin's paramour, Edna Purviance to say that Peavey had discovered Taylor's dead body. Immediately, the William Desmond Taylor murder became a cause célèbre, with a line-up of suspects, but little in the way of motive. There was no sign of a break-in or robbery. What a neighbour believed to be a car backfiring the previous evening shortly after Normand left was identified as the fatal shot, while the same neighbour claimed to have seen a mysterious man on Taylor's porch. Could this have been a crime of passion and was Normand the one who'd pulled the trigger? Then there was 22-year-old Mary Minter, who was apparently being groomed by Taylor as a movie starlet and may have been sexually involved with the director from before she reached maturity. The missing secretary – who had convictions for embezzlement and forgery – had left Taylor's employment seven months before, but quit his job and vanished on that fateful first day of February. African-American Henry Peavey also joined the list of suspects... Here was a Hollywood scandal that would eclipse the Arbuckle story in complexity!

Taylor had been born William Cunningham Deane-Tanner in Carlow, Ireland. He came to the United States in 1890, aged 18, and a short acting career in New York City followed. He married the daughter of a wealthy Wall Street broker who provided Taylor with funding to set up a business, allowing him to quit acting. The pair featured in New York society until he abruptly vanished in 1908 at the age of 36, deserting his wife and daughter (born in 1903). Changing his name to William Desmond Taylor, he moved to Hollywood and worked as an actor once more in the new film industry before moving behind the camera and making his first film as director, *The Awakening* (1915).

Stories of a possible secret romance between Normand and Taylor caused Mack Sennett to be questioned about the murder, his motive jealousy. Studio head Adolph Zukor, who'd often employed Taylor, offered a reward of $2,500 for information leading to the arrest of his killer. Of course, the Hearst press who'd done so much to sink the career of Arbuckle had a field day with the Taylor case.

Countless police, private investigators and keen amateurs were soon examining every aspect of the case as the stories about William Desmond Taylor – true, false and indeterminate – began to multiply. Was the mystery man on the porch actually a mystery woman – maybe Mary Minter's outraged mother, Charlotte Shelby, avenging her daughter's honour? Did Paramount Studios' general manager Charles Eyton have more involvement in the mystery than the clean-up job he and associates were alleged to have engaged in, removing evidence of Taylor's sexual connections with several up-and-coming Hollywood actresses and actors...?

As time went on, the theories became ever more outlandish, mainly due to the lack of clear evidence and obvious suspects. Taylor was variously seen as the victim of a drug-related hit (he was helping Normand kick cocaine and had contact with her suppliers), as a practitioner of black magic who'd fallen foul of demonic forces or part of a powerful Hollywood homosexual cabal that had decided he was too high profile and reckless. However, the two most plausible candidates in this ever more implausible tale remained either Normand (jealous of Taylor's other affairs) or Sennett (jealous of Normand's affair with Taylor).

No-one was ever charged, but many Hollywood figures were tarnished by their mere connection with the William Desmond Taylor scandal. Normand's drug use didn't help the decline in her fortunes, but the Taylor case hastened her fall from grace. She died in 1930 from tuberculosis and the effects of her drug addiction. Sennett desperately tried to turn the spotlight away from himself, knowing the possible effect on his business, and consistently claimed that if the police could find the mysterious secretary Sands (who may even have been Taylor's brother Dennis using an assumed identity!), then the mystery would be solved. Neither happened. A bungled police investigation resulted in the loss of evidence and poor record keeping, leaving the field of suspects open and the case officially unsolved to this day.

The William Desmond Taylor murder, following so rapidly on the heels of the Fatty Arbuckle case, fuelled the calls for the filmmaking community to clean up its act. It wouldn't be the last time.

OLIVE THOMAS (1894-1920)

On 10 September 1920, the 25-year-old Selznick Pictures star Olive Thomas was discovered dead and naked in a hotel room in Paris. She'd apparently committed suicide by taking poison. Following her death, rumours spread of orgies and out-of-control drug-fuelled Hollywood parties. According to the newspapers, Thomas was dead due to her decadent Hollywood lifestyle, a lifestyle that should be curbed before it spread nationwide. Connected to newly created Hollywood 'royalty', Thomas was married to Jack Pickford, brother of the movies' then-biggest star Mary Pickford. The oration at her memorial was delivered by director William Desmond Taylor, who was soon-to-be-murdered himself. She'd appeared in a film alongside Virginia Rappé, the 'victim' in the Arbuckle case. Thomas' death was silent Hollywood's first major scandal, but the fact that it took place abroad gave the industry a chance to attempt to publicly distance itself from responsibility; the blame was to be shifted to the decadent nightlife of Paris.

Oliveretta Elaine Duffy was born at Charleroi, Pennsylvania, on 20 October 1894. In her early teens she was working in a department store, before going to New York and becoming an artists' model, posing for Harrison Fisher and others. A letter of recommendation from Fisher to Florenz Ziegfeld resulted in a position in the 'Midnight Frolic' show in 1915. She continued appearing in the Ziegfeld shows until 1917, and rumours suggested an affair between the pair. Married to and then divorced from Bernard Krug Thomas, she then married Jack Pickford in 1917.

Thomas started in movies in 1916, appearing in the 10th episode of silent serial *Beatrice Fairfax*, signing to the Triangle Film Corporation and featuring in comedies for Harry Fox. A series of shorts followed through the four years she worked in movies, including *Tom Sawyer* (1917) and

Youthful Folly (1920), for which she also wrote the original storyline. However, Thomas – on the basis of the films she made up to 1920 – would have been entirely forgotten today if it had not been for the scandal caused by her untimely death, aged 25.

Unsolved, it remains controversial to this day. After a quarrel with her husband Jack Pickford, she mixed 'syphilis medication' with alcohol and drank it. The official verdict was accidental death: she'd mistaken the medicine for a 'sleeping potion'. Taken to the American Hospital at Neuilly-sur-Seine, there was time for her condition to be reported in the *New York Herald* (Paris edition) on 9 September 1920. The report focused on her 'domestic difficulties' with her husband, suggesting this was at the root of her suicide bid. Thomas died with Pickford at her bedside on 10 September, and a French police investigation followed. A former American army captain named 'Spalding' or 'Spaulding', who was facing six months' imprisonment for cocaine smuggling, was questioned as part of the investigation.

Police Commissioner Catrou, assigned to examine the circumstances of Thomas' death, returned a finding of accidental death. An autopsy seemed to officially confirm the verdict. Arriving in London several days later, Pickford claimed (quoted in the *Los Angeles Examiner* of 13 September 1920): 'Her death is a ghastly mistake. We were the happiest couple imaginable',[11] contrary to other reports of their turbulent marriage.

THOMAS HARPER (H.) INCE (1882-1924)

A film pioneer, alongside DW Griffith and Cecil B. DeMille, Thomas H. Ince is recalled for the mystery surrounding his death rather than for any of his films. Ince started in vaudeville but bypassed acting to move straight into film, directing briefly at Biograph, before pioneering the Western as a recognisable genre alongside William S. Hart. He bought land in California to create a special ranch exclusively for shooting movies. He then directed his first feature film, *The Battle of Gettysburg* in 1914, before teaming up with DW Griffith and Mack Sennett to form Triangle in 1915.

Ince gave up directing, moving instead into production, as he'd always been more interested in the marketing and selling of films than in the actual creation of them.

Working at a variety of studios and with a host of talent through the mid-1920s, it's safe to say that Ince made his fair share of enemies, but who did he cross that badly that they wanted to shoot him? Invited to a party aboard William Randolph Hearst's yacht in November 1924, Ince joined Hearst's mistress Marion Davies, Charlie Chaplin, Elinor Glyn and young gossip columnist Louella Parsons on the *Oneida* for a trip off the California coast. It remains unclear to this day exactly what happened, but Ince was taken off the boat at San Diego and died two days later. The official explanation: heart failure, following severe indigestion. Rumours abounded of drink and drugs on board, and that either Ince or Chaplin had made a pass at Davies. In his film based on the case, *The Cat's Meow* (2001), writer-director Peter Bogdanovich speculated that Ince was killed by a fatal shot in the back, fired by Hearst who'd mistaken him for Chaplin, who in turn had been flirting with Davies. This complicated web makes for a great movie, but it seems unlikely that so long after the event that any satisfactory solution will be presented.

These selected silent scandals were not the only prominent cases in the Hollywood of the teens and 1920s, and they certainly wouldn't be the last. From the moment actress Peg Entwistle leapt into Hollywood folklore on 8 September 1932 by throwing herself from the H in the Hollywood sign, it has been a venue for symbolic, nation-defining scandals. In turn, the morals of the movie colony have been regularly censored and controlled by government action. From the inception of the film business to the dawn of the digital era, some things have never changed...

INTERNATIONAL SILENT CINEMA

Just as film production spread across Europe and was beginning to consolidate into a semi-industrial business, World War I decimated the industry. The growing American film business came to dominance worldwide, almost unchallenged. With no language barrier to prevent access to American movies, clowns like Charlie Chaplin and dramatic stars like Mary Pickford and Douglas Fairbanks were as well known in France and Spain as they were in New York and Chicago. Even after the war, with audiences now used to longer films featuring specific stars, it would prove to be very difficult for national cinemas to re-establish themselves. From the Hollywood point-of-view, recovering their costs at home was central to their business model so all overseas exploitation was additional income. It would be the end of the twentieth century before this business model had to change significantly.

GERMANY

Before World War I, Germany's film industry was not terribly strong. Exports were limited, while imports, mainly from Hollywood, dominated. Cinema had been criticised prior to the war as immoral, an unwelcome lowbrow competitor to live theatre. In the years immediately prior to the war, attitudes to the film business were changing as writers, directors and actors from theatre began to take film more seriously. The result was bigger audiences for movie stars like Paul Wegener (seen in the Faustian tale *The Student of Prague*, 1913). Actresses Henny Porten and the

Danish Asta Nielsen were also on the verge of international fame when the export and import of films were banned in 1916.

Germany retained a strong and vital film production business during the war years, especially as the import of American films discontinued until 1920. The German government supported the growth of a uniquely German film industry. Even when American imports resumed, films from Hollywood proved to be too expensive for local distributors due to currency exchange difficulties. In the post-war years, lavish costume dramas proved to be central to the German film business, giving rise to the career of Ernst Lubitsch with films like *Madame Dubarry* (1919) and *Anna Boleyn* (1920).

The biggest development in the German industry in the 1920s, until the coming of sound, was German Expressionism. Between 1918 and the rise of Hitler in 1933, the German film industry was second only to Hollywood in size and influence. With no imports until after 1920, the national industry had a chance to blossom. The emergence of the production power base of UFA (Universum Film Aktiengesellschaft) gave rise to a distinctive German film style, defined by its melodrama and lighting. Films such as *The Golem* (with Paul Wegener, 1920), *The Cabinet of Dr Caligari* (1920) and FW Murnau's *Nosferatu* (1922) gave rise to the Expressionist movement in cinema. Featuring stylised sets and equally stylised acting, painted backdrops, phantasmagoria realised on screen, dream-like images and incoherent narratives, these films were non-naturalistic and unique. For most of the 1920s, it was to be the dominant cinematic style in Germany, a distinctive movement, producing around two-dozen films between 1920 and 1927. Films like *Dr. Mabuse der Spieler* (*Dr. Mabuse the Gambler*, 1922), *Wachsfigurenkabinett* (*Waxworks*, 1924) and *Orlacs Hände* (*The Hands of Orlac*, 1924) made the settings, backgrounds, editing and camerawork as important as the performances of the actors. The movement essentially ended with Fritz Lang's *Metropolis* (1927). As the political atmosphere in Germany changed, many directors (like Lang), actors and others fled for new careers in Hollywood. The coming of sound cinema in Germany was corrupted by the influence of the Nazi ideology and the outbreak of World War II.

ITALY

From 1910 onwards, Italian cinema boomed. Italian exports were seen widely, with easily understood historical dramas like *Quo Vadis?* (1913) and *Cabiria* (1914) laying the groundwork for the ongoing association between Italy and epic cinema. *Cabiria* was set in the Roman Empire, and told a story of personal strife, kidnapping and sacrifice set against a background of such spectacles as erupting volcanoes and collapsing temples. Alongside these epics, Italy's industry also produced a series of famous actresses, known as the country's 'divas', including Lyda Borelli (*Ma l'amor mio non muore!/'But My Love Does Not Die!'*, 1913) and her rival Francesca Bertini (*Assunta Spina*, 1915).

Italy united much of its film production capacity in 1919 under the Unione Cinematografica Italiana (UCI) and followed the German model of lush costume dramas, only to find they did not seem to appeal to Italian audiences. The UCI endured until 1925 when a remake of *Quo Vadis?* almost ruined the domestic Italian industry, with many directors departing to work in the more prosperous cinema industries in France and Germany.

FRANCE

Having virtually invented cinema through the work of the Lumiére Brothers, it's not surprising that the French were second only to English-speaking America and Britain in recognising filmmaking as an entertainment business. It was this willingness to produce and export films that caused the French industry to falter prior to World War I, which virtually halted production. The Pathé Brothers attempted, from 1913, to take on the big American distributors at their own game. Initially they succeeded in exporting shorts and serials like *The Perils of Pauline* (1914, which made a star of Pearl White), but lost out in the move to features. Rival company Gaumont suffered a similar fate, capitalising for a while on the serial work of director Louis Feuillade (Fantomas, 1913-1914, *Les Vampires*, 1915, and *Judex*, 1916) before the war ended production on virtually all films except newsreels. Exceptions were made for patriotic films such as 1917's *Mères Françaises* (*French Mothers*).

During the 1920s, over 70 per cent of the French film market was dominated by American-produced movies. Local production had all but collapsed. With limited production there was limited opportunity to continue the export strategy that had served the industry well in the pre-war years. As with Expressionism in Germany, France developed a distinctive national cinema style dubbed French Impressionism. This consisted of using cinematic techniques to convey sensation and emotional impressions. Abel Gance was one of the first directors to explore this territory in his musical drama *La Dixième symphonie* (1918), only to develop it in longer and more costly films like *J'accuse* (1919) and *La Roue* (1922). It was with the widely acclaimed *Napoléon* (1927) that the French Impressionist film movement reached its climax. The last reel of Gance's film was shot with three cameras side-by-side and projected onto a trio of screens to create a triptych image, a widescreen innovation that wouldn't be attempted again until 70mm movies or gimmicks like Cinerama in the late 1960s.

Other Impressionist directors, such as Marcel L'Herbier (*Rose-France*, 1919), Jean Epstein (*La Glace à trois faces/The Three-Sided Mirror*, 1927) and Jean Renoir (*La Petite marchande d'allumettes/The Little Match Girl*, 1928), son of painter Auguste Renoir, developed the style. Among them, they developed cinema as the personal expression of the artist, creating experience and emotion for the spectator. Mostly working within commercial narrative forms, the French Impressionists would occasionally delve into the worlds of the avant-garde.

By the end of the 1920s, most of the techniques developed in French Impressionist filmmaking had been absorbed by the mainstream industry in Hollywood, making the French approach less distinct. Certain directors were driven in a more avant-garde experimental direction as a result, while the coming of sound also contributed to the end of an era in French film as costs increased dramatically and the business became much more corporate.

RUSSIA

During World War I, the Russian film industry developed largely in isolation, just as it had in Germany. Pre-war, Russian cinema was dominated by the French Pathé company, which opened a studio in Russia in 1908. In the following years other foreign companies like Gaumont entered the territory, and by 1914, and the dawn of World War I, the Russian film industry was developing well, producing comedies, melodramas and thrillers. Although imported films were popular, local talent was finding an audience. Russia's entry into the war in July 1914 brought an immediate embargo on non-Russian films.

The Russian Revolution of 1917 led to the development of a national cinema with a clear ideological purpose, a medium to be used to 'educate' and 'enlighten' the proletariat population. Famously, Russia developed a unique distribution system known as `agit-trains', consisting of trains kitted out with film screening facilities that would travel from town to town and screen Communist propaganda to local audiences. Nationalised in August 1919, the Russian industry was overseen by Lenin's wife. Lenin himself stated in 1922 that, 'Of all the arts, for us the cinema is the most important.'[12]

The work of two directors in particular dominated Russian silent cinema of the 1920s: Eisenstein and Pudovkin. Shortage of film stock meant that only a handful of cinema practitioners had access to the means of production. Montage, or editing with political meaning, became the dominant force in Russian cinema. Sergei Eisenstein directed *Strike* (1924), a film which featured the working proletariat as a whole as its 'hero'. Using contrasting editing, Eisenstein juxtaposed the situation of the rich and the poor, and built a dynamic portrayal of the massacre of the workers by the repressive authorities. His next film, *Battleship Potemkin* (1925) was made to celebrate the failed 1905 revolution, focusing on two events – the Odessa sailors' rebellion and the reprisals by the Tsar. The emotional impact of the film derived from Eisenstein's approach to montage, colliding two images to create a new third, deeper meaning. *October* (1927), made for the anniversary of the 1917 Revolution, extended his montage techniques and brought them to bear on the portrayal of characters, undermining the position of Kerensky, leader of the provisional Government. Eisenstein ended up looking for work in Hollywood, failed to find any and relocated to Mexico to work on the never completed *Que Viva Mexico!* He returned to filmmaking in Russian in the late-1930s when he completed sound films such as *Alexander Nevsky* (1938) and *Ivan the Terrible* (1948), with the unfinished Part II released in 1958, ten years after Eisenstein's death.

Vsevolod Pudovkin was inspired to make movies by DW Griffith's *Intolerance* (a copy was smuggled into Russia in 1919), resulting in *Mother* (1926) and *The End of St Petersburg* (1927). Less involved in the dour realism of much of Russian didactive cinema, Pudovkin created the lush and lyrical *Storm Over Asia* (1928).

OTHER COUNTRIES

A basic introduction to the topic of silent cinema such as this cannot expand upon all the individual national cinemas of the period 1919-1928. In addition to those detailed, there were significant filmic developments in the Scandinavian countries and the far east of Japan, also in countries like Mexico, India and New Zealand. Scandinavian cinema focused on natural and urban locations, dramatic lighting effects and lengthy dramas. August Blom's psychological melodrama, inspired by the sinking of the Titanic, *Atlantis* (1913), was at eight reels the longest Danish film to that date. Forest Holger-Madsen made *The Evangelist* (1914), a prison drama featuring a framing story and lengthy flashbacks. As a neutral country, Danish cinema flourished during the war years. The Swedish industry boomed during the same period, with the varied work of Af Klercker in comedies, thrillers, melodrama and war films being particularly notable. Actor Victor Sjöström moved behind the camera, introducing a more restrained acting style and bringing naturalism to Swedish silent cinema, making it the only real international alternative to Hollywood in the postwar years. Silent cinema was prolonged in Japan much longer than elsewhere, with live narrators still required right into the 1930s. Resistant to Western influences, Japan was slow to adapt to new technological, stylistic and production techniques, sticking with tried-and-tested methods, much as Chaplin would in Hollywood. Slow to adopt technological change, Japanese silent cinema flourished artistically for a longer period than in the West, producing a distinct and influential body of work still being explored by scholars today.

By the end of the 1920s, silent cinema was a distinct, internationally successful art form. Storytelling and cinematic techniques had developed markedly from the previous decade when the industry had been dominated by technical innovation and cinema's artistic struggle to keep up with these developments. The now stable technology and the distinct national cinemas that developed alongside the international exchange of cinema (interrupted by World War I), had contributed enormously. The coming of sound, however, as explored in Chapter 11, was to see silent cinema as a distinctive art form come to an abrupt end.

THE SILENT CLASSICS

Le Voyage dans la lune/A Trip to the Moon (1902)

Directed by: George Méliès
Country: France
Cast: Georges Méliès, members of the Châtelet Ballet/Folies Bergère

One of the earliest science fiction films, *Le Voyage dans la lune* gave the world the iconic image of the moon (complete with face) with a giant rocket ship embedded in its left eye. Méliès' loose version of the 1865 Jules Verne story *From the Earth to the Moon* (with elements from HG Wells' then new *First Men in the Moon*, 1901) was the 400th film the inventive director had made. It cost him 10,000 Francs, a large investment, but Méliès had amassed enough experience by then to know that he'd make that back and more in distributing his film, before the inevitable pirate copies began circulating. The film charts the journey of a group of Victorian explorers on a joyride to the moon and is a whimsical narrative notable for its invention of a host of fascinating cinematic techniques, without which much of the history of cinema would not have been possible. Méliès developed the art of special effects through many of his films, including double exposures, performers (often himself) acting with themselves through split screens, and dissolves and fades. Méliès also pioneered film editing by linking individual reels together. The backgrounds were simple, painted theatrical flats. Méliès' movie has all the elements of the modern science fiction blockbuster, from adventurous scientists, a trip through space, unbelievable special effects and life forms from far-away lands and planets.

The Birth of a Nation (1915)

Directed by: DW Griffith
Country: USA
Cast: Ralph Lewis, Lillian Gish, Elmer Clifton, Robert Harron, Miriam Cooper, Mae Marsh, Walter Long

Still controversial almost 100 years later, Griffith's openly racist epic is a product of its time. Based on the 1905 play *The Clansman*, the film charts the creation of the USA and is regarded as perhaps the single most important American film in the development of cinema technique. While Griffith did not invent all the techniques on display in *The Birth of a Nation*, he did refine and develop ideas such as sequential and parallel editing, night photography, outdoor shooting, colour tinting, moving cameras, iris and fade-out effects, dissolves, panoramic shots and many more. This one film brought together many of the basics of cinematic technique that remains unchanged today. At three hours and an eventual cost of in excess of $100,000, this was the biggest film of its era. The controversy the film sparked in its portrayal of black Americans remains to this day, with its position at #44 on the American Film Institute's Top 100 and controversial selection for the US National Film Registry in the mid-1990s. Despite the problems of its content, the film is still important as the foundation of modern cinematic style.

Intolerance (1916)

Directed by: DW Griffith
Country: USA
Cast: Lillian Gish, Robert Harron, Mae Marsh, Fred Turner

Often considered the single greatest film of the silent era, Griffith's *Intolerance* avoids the political controversies of *The Birth of a Nation* and further develops that film's cinematic techniques. Essentially a time-tripping soap opera, the film featured four different time periods, and the trials and tribulations of love and relationships. Buster Keaton's *Three Ages* (1923) effectively spoofs Griffith's masterpiece. Tackling the theme of social injustice through the ages, *Intolerance* began with a 'contemporary' 1914 sequence (about a wrongly convicted Catholic), before exploring conditions in AD27 (the story of Christ), AD1572 (the persecution of the Huguenots) and 539BC (the fall of Babylon). Griffith effectively introduces non-linear storytelling, jumping between parallel events in each time zone, with each individual story illuminating the overall themes of injustice, hypocrisy, hatred and persecution. Lillian Gish's cradle rocking 'everywoman' links the sequences together.

The most expensive film of its time, with some estimates close to $2 million, *Intolerance* was a commercial flop, failing to captivate an audience unused to the intricate narrative that unfolded. The cost of the Babylonian sections became an early byword for Hollywood excess, as did Griffith's insistence on full orchestral accompaniment wherever the film was screened. The seeming pacifism of the film was also out-of-step with audiences facing the carnage of World War I. Crane shots, epic crowd scenes and live animals all advanced filmmaking as Griffith further consolidated his claim to be the 'inventor' of cinema.

Broken Blossoms (1919)

Directed by: DW Griffith
Country: USA
Cast: Lillian Gish, Richard Barthelmess, Donald Crisp

Griffith once again directs Gish, this time as tragic Cockney waif Lucy Burrows. Gish delivers one of cinema's most melodramatic performances, regarded as quaint today, but central to the style of cinema at the time. The film relates the story of a seemingly mystical, fragile romance in London's foggy slums between a young, gentle, opium-addicted Chinese man (Barthelmess) and an illegitimate waif (Gish), who is abused and

ultimately killed by her bigoted prize-fighting father (Crisp). Much smaller in scale and ambition than either *The Birth of a Nation* or *Intolerance*, in *Broken Blossoms* Griffith brought all his considerable cinematic technique to bear on a personal tragic story based around the relationships between three main characters. Adapted from Thomas Burke's book *Limehouse Nights*, the film revolves around the performance by Gish that laid the foundation of much movie acting in the silent era. The controversial, soap opera subject matter drew audiences to *Broken Blossoms* just as the serious epic of *Intolerance* had put them off. Taking place almost entirely in just two small, contained interior sets, and shot in a simple soft-focus style (by cinematographer Henrick Sartov), this intimate drama was filmed over three weeks and on a modest budget, proving that Griffith was a master of more than just the overblown cinema epic.

Das Kabinett des Dr. Caligari
The Cabinet of Dr. Caligari (1920)

Directed by: Robert Wiene
Country: Germany
Cast: Friedrich Feher, Hans Heinrich, Werner Krauss, Conrad Veidt, Lil Dagover

Extremely influential on the developing genre of 1930s' horror cinema (particularly the Universal cycle of monster movies), the German expressionist classic *The Cabinet of Dr. Caligari* also had long-lasting influence on the post-World War II genre of film noir. A young man, Francis, recounts a tale of murder in which the death of his friend Alan is predicted by hypnotised sleepwalker Cesare, part of Dr. Caligari's travelling fair. Is Caligari controlling Cesare and having him commit murder? The twist at the end of the film, revealing that the narrator, Francis, in whom the audience has put its faith, is in fact unreliable (he is a patient in Dr. Caligari's asylum), was brand new at the time and incredibly influential. Owing something to Paul Wegener's *The Student of Prague* (1913), Caligari brought dream-like expressionist style to the screen in its extreme sets which loomed above the characters at all angles. The film originally had intertitles shot in an angular style consistent with the film's bizarre sets. The subjective perception of the film's unreliable narrator is reflected in the uncanny appearance of the world in which the film takes place. Nothing, from the acting to the make-up, escapes the expressionist touch. The possible poetry of silent cinema was revealed by the dream world of *The Cabinet of Dr. Caligari*.

Der Golem, wie er in die Welt kam
The Golem (How He Came into the World) (1920)

Directed by: Paul Wegener
Country: Germany
Cast: Paul Wegener, Albert Steinruck, Lyda Salmonova

Der Golem is possibly the first great monster movie. This was actually the third time director-star Paul Wegener had played the title creature, his earlier efforts (now lost) being rough drafts for his final, more elaborate drama based upon the original Jewish legend. His first version (*Der Golem*, 1914) was a contemporary-set tale in which an antique dealer revives the 400-year-old creature. The second (*The Golem and the Dancer*, 1917) was a comedy in which a man (Wegener), after seeing the 1914 *Der Golem* in a cinema, dresses up as the creature to frighten a dancer (Salmanova) in what may be the horror genre's first ironic sequel. The final 1920 version is a prequel, and tells the origins of the Golem. When the Emperor decrees that the Jews of medieval Prague should be evicted from the ghetto, mystical Rabbi Loew creates a clay giant and summons the demon Astaroth who animates the Golem. Intended as a protector, the golem's purpose is twisted and the 'monster' terrorises the guilty and innocent alike, until a little girl ingenuously ends his reign of fear. Wegener's golem is an impressive creation, a pre-*Frankenstein* (1930) lumbering creature with simple intentions. While modern audiences may regard the Golem creature as more comical than frightening, the film remains an unusual cinematic retelling of a folk story.

The Kid (1921)

Directed by: Charles Chaplin
Country: USA
Cast: Charlie Chaplin, Jackie Coogan, Edna Purviance, Albert Austin

Chaplin's little tramp inherits an abandoned baby ('misplaced' by unwed mother Purviance) that he reluctantly commits to looking after. Five years on, the kid and the tramp have formed a criminal partnership, relying on each other to survive in a harsh world. Their main scam involves the youngster smashing windows before Chaplin's glazier turns up to offer his services in repairing them. Finally, the tramp has to battle the authorities that want to take the kid to an orphanage. It's the evident on-screen relationship between Chaplin and young Coogan (later Uncle Fester in *The Addam's Family*) which makes *The Kid* so successful. Always a slow worker, Chaplin's first full-length feature film caused his studio First National much angst as he took almost a year to make the film, reworking sequences and deepening the emotional, melodramatic content. As much a drama of life on the streets as a comedy, heavily influenced by Chaplin's own London experiences, *The Kid* was to provide a model for much of his later feature film work. A critical and commercial success upon release, it grossed over $2.5 million at the US box office. *The Kid* is easily the pinnacle of Chaplin's career, an ideal and continually appealing combination of the great comic's humour and pathos.

Häxan/Witchcraft Through the Ages (1922)

Directed by: Benjamin Christensen
Country: Sweden
Cast: Benjamin Christensen, Astrid Holm, Karen Winther, Maren Pedersen

No-one seems quite sure what the unique film *Häxan* was intended to be: a documentary, a horror film or a comedy? Modern audiences (and critics) often believe that graphic horror on screen began in the late 1950s-early 1960s. The images in Häxan prove otherwise. Ahead of its time in

breaking taboos, and in combining the barely recognised genres of documentary and horror film, *Häxan* was the result of two years spent by director Benjamin Christensen researching the supernatural and the history of witchcraft. At a time in history when science was coming to dominate public discourse, Christensen wanted to look back to an earlier age when superstition dominated human thought. In the light of today's knowledge, the film does get caught up in the then (1920s) current obsession with Freudian analysis, but it is a significant step forward for the cinematic arts. It is caught in an uncomfortable position: on the one hand, it tries to be a serious analysis of history, yet its images have more in common with the later genre of supernatural exploitation films. So, is *Häxan* high art or trash cinema, or both?

A contemporary review of the film in Hollywood's trade paper *Variety* noted: 'Wonderful though this picture is, it is absolutely unfit for public exhibition.'[13] Christensen stages elaborate recreations of supernatural stories that dominated medieval witchcraft scares, scaring through brief glimpses of horror, knowing that the human mind would fill in the blanks with images worse than anything the screen could conjure. *Häxan* is horror excused on screen as 'education', a gambit many less accomplished films and filmmakers would follow years later.

Nosferatu, eine Symphonie des Grauens
Nosferatu, A Symphony of Horrors (1922)

Directed by: FW Murnau
Country: Germany
Cast: Max Schreck, Gustav von Wangenheim, Greta Schröder, Alexander Granach

Nosferatu is the first and, perhaps, most faithful film version of Bram Stoker's novel *Dracula*, made a decade before the official Bela Lugosi version. As an unauthorised adaptation of the immensely popular novel, Murnau changed the character names (Count Dracula became Count Orlok) and other details to avoid legal entanglements. That wasn't enough to protect the film from Stoker's widow who endeavoured to have every print destroyed: it's sheer luck that the movie has survived to be recognised as a classic of the horror genre. Max Schreck's depiction of a vampire was as a more animalistic character than the urbane Lugosi Count. This is a cinematic vampire from a time before bloodsuckers had become a well-worn cliché. The art direction by Murnau's collaborator, Albin Grau, gave this world of (then) unthinkable horror a unique look that would influence the genre for decades to come. The basic story, of a doomed estate agent's trip to the Carpathian Mountains and a vampire's return trip to England, remains as in the novel. Gripping images abound, from the intercutting of two simultaneous events (Orlok advancing upon his prey while a woman sleepwalks towards them) to the scenes of Orlok on the ship. Murnau captures the viewers' dark fears upon the screen, relying less on Hitchcock-style jumps and tension, and more on the belief that evil things lurk just around the corner.

Safety Last (1923)

Directed by: Fred Newmeyer and Sam Taylor
Country: USA
Cast: Harold Lloyd, Mildred Davis, Bill Strother, Westcott B. Clarke

Prime among Harold Lloyd's 'daredevil' movies, *Safety Last* is largely re-membered for the iconic image of Lloyd scaling a department store and hanging from the hands of a clock face. Although he did indeed climb tall buildings in several shorts and features, the majority of his films didn't include such daredevil antics. Here, Harold has gone to the city to make good in order to get Mildred (Davis, later Lloyd's real-life wife) to marry him. Working in a lowly department store job, he tries to impress by passing himself off as a mystery man who's been scaling public build-ings, only to find himself trapped into doing the feat for real. Inspired by the 1920s vogue for 'human flies' (cast member Bill Strother was one in real life and partially inspired the film), *Safety Last*'s building ascent was developed from several earlier Lloyd shorts and came to dominate a film that contains many quieter moments and fine comic business. The sets were built in dramatic high locations that gave the illusion of extreme danger in total safety; the 20-minute climax to the movie appeals as much to audiences today as it did back in the 1920s. The comic inventiveness that went into the incidents and props Lloyd encounters during the climb has never been bettered.

It's little remembered today that Harold Lloyd was a bigger box office draw than Chaplin or Keaton, producing 11 features during the 1920s in contrast to Chaplin's four.

The Iron Horse (1924)

Directed by: John Ford
Country: USA
Cast: Cyril Chadwick, George O'Brien, Madge Bellamy

John Ford is known largely as a director of classic Westerns such as *Stagecoach* (1939), *My Darling Clementine* (1946), *Fort Apache* (1948) and *The Searchers* (1956). It should come as no surprise, then, that one of his earliest significant films was also a Western. *The Iron Horse* is an epic about the creation of the first railway line from the east to the west coasts of the US, which was completed in 1869. It's Ford's celebration of the end of the frontier due to the arrival of the railway, which allowed the industrial and commercial development of the western half of America.

The film was made on location in the Sierra Nevada and included 10,000 cattle and 1,300 buffalo among the cast. Ford tracked down two original engines, the Jupiter and the 116, that had appeared in Andrew Russell's famous photograph of the joining of the tracks at Promontory Point, Utah. Ford re-creates the real-life scene with the actual trains, posing his cast as in the photograph. *The Iron Horse* depicts the struggle to open the West and the lives that were lost in the process, as well as the lives of those who got rich from the railway. Temporary towns spring up around the ongoing laying of the tracks, and are abandoned as the work and workers move on. *The Iron Horse* may not be as flashy as Ford's later work or as accomplished as some other 'arty' silent movies, but it does capture the sense of struggle that was the early history of America.

Sherlock Jr. (1924)

Directed by: Buster Keaton
Country: USA
Cast: Buster Keaton, Kathryn McGuire, Ward Crane

Keaton plays a cinema projectionist who dreams of being a detective: literally, as a dream takes him through the screen and into the detective movie (the idea that caused Keaton to make the movie). Dream logic dominates this film, so the impossible becomes unexpectedly commonplace – doorsteps turn into vases, or Buster is suddenly dumped into the middle of the road. Film grammar also plays a part, as editing takes Buster immediately from a cliff to a confrontation with a lion to the middle of the desert. Investigating the theft of a pearl necklace (reflecting real-life troubles), he ends up sitting on the handlebars of a rider-less motorbike, hurtling through the streets until he rescues the film's heroine. During the shooting Keaton unknowingly suffered a broken neck that only came to light over a decade later. Keaton reckoned it had happened when a water tower was used to blow him off the top of a train in *Sherlock, Jr.*

The film-within-a-film gambit was wonderfully original and endlessly repeated in films such as Woody Allen's *The Purple Rose of Cairo* (1985). *Sherlock Jr.* was something of a collection of many of the routines Keaton had learned in vaudeville, ingeniously adapted for the screen. It was also, up to this point, Keaton's most technically challenging film. The screen upon which the film was seemingly projected was, in fact, a stage set lit to look like film. *Sherlock Jr.* was the film that Roscoe 'Fatty' Arbuckle was set to direct when the Virginia Rappé scandal broke (see Chapter 8). So distracted by the fuss was Arbuckle that Keaton had to take him off the picture after a few weeks. It took five months to make, but due to bad reactions at early previews, Keaton recut it, then always remained dissatisfied with the structure. Despite that, *Sherlock Jr.* is one of the greatest films about the way audiences experience and become involved in the magic of the movies.

The Thief of Bagdad (1924)

Directed by: Raoul Walsh
Country: USA
Cast: Douglas Fairbanks, Julanne Johnston, Anna May Wong

At his dashing best, Douglas Fairbanks finds himself on a magical quest in this Arabian Nights-inspired fantasy. Julanne Johnston is the Princess who captures Fairbanks' heart after he poses as a Prince and enjoys a ride on his magic carpet. In order to win her, he has to embark on a quest for a magical chest and then overthrow a corrupt ruler, using the chest's magical properties. This is one of the longer mainstream silent movies and boasts some fantastic settings designed by William Cameron Menzies (later a quixotic movie designer and director who would work on Alexander Korda's 1940 remake). This was a costly film, at over $2 million. Underappreciated in its time, it has since come to be seen as one of the more significant silent movies, for its sense of adventure, magical special effects and exotic settings. Everything seems vast and impressive. However, Fairbanks was stung by its failure and retreated to more straightforward swashbuckling roles.

Alongside *Caligari*, *The Thief of Bagdad* draws attention to the importance of the art of film design. The determination to make Bagdad a seemingly ephemeral city, a mere backdrop to the action, and the methods of realising the special effects like flying carpets were co-ordinated by Fairbanks (as producer and star) in conjunction with his designers, such as Menzies. It's undoubtedly an Art Director's movie, and Raoul Walsh had little input into the mise-en-scène of the finished product.

Greed (1924)

Directed by: Erich von Stroheim
Country: USA
Cast: Gibson Gowland, ZaSu Pitts, Jean Hersholt, Chester Conklin

Greed was another box office failure at the time of its release, which has since been recognised as a significant film. This dark study of corruption features three main characters: McTeague, a San Francisco dentist, his miserable wife, Trina, and their treacherous mutual friend, Marcus. Their downfall is brought about by their lust for gold. Based upon Frank Norris' best-selling novel of the gold rush era, *McTeague*, Von Stroheim's film took nine months to shoot and a further fifteen months to shape through editing. The director's bizarre ambition to faithfully adapt every page of the novel (even though he shifted the setting to a post-1906 earthquake San Francisco) accounted for the film's initially insane length of forty-

seven reels (a reel being ten-twelve minutes long). The use of authentic locations also caused many production problems. Von Stroheim's second cut came in at forty-two reels (still a seven hour movie!). A fraction of the original film remains today, running for two-and-a-quarter hours (ten reels, a quarter of its original length). The edited original negatives were probably melted down by MGM to extract the silver nitrate: somehow suitable given the character's greed for gold. In the original release prints, gold objects were hand-tinted to stand out. In later years, Von Stroheim was reduced to playing caricatured gimmicky parts such as Gloria Swanson's butler in *Sunset Boulevard* (1950) and the camp commandant in *La Grande Illusion* (1937).

The Freshman (1925)

Directed by: Sam Taylor and Fred Newmeyer
Country: USA
Cast: Harold Lloyd, Jobyna Rolston, Pat Harmon

Lloyd plays Harold Lamb (nicknamed 'Speedy'), a college freshman who models his behaviour on his film heroes before he prepares to make his debut at college. En route, he hooks up with Peggy (Rolston), a coat-check girl, and stays at her mother's boarding house. At college, his forced enthusiasm brings him nothing but ridicule, although he believes himself to be popular. Hearing that true popularity comes from joining the football team, Lamb tries out, only to be relegated to the role of waterboy. As his team are losing a vital game, however, 'Speedy' gets his chance to impress, taking to the field and winning the game. *The Freshman* is one of Lloyd's best-known films and he would go on to star in a Preston Sturges-directed pseudo-sequel *The Sin of Harold Dibbledock* (aka *Mad Wednesday*, 1947).

The original intention was to shoot the concluding football game first (as in *Safety Last*, where the climatic building climb was shot first and the rest of the plot worked out later). However, Lloyd decided that it was important that his college kid character develop and change through the film, and the only way to do that was to shoot in continuity. This new emphasis on character saw Lloyd developing his films away from an endless string of gags to a more rounded picture.

The Freshman has been selected for preservation in the United States National Film Registry and is widely regarded as Lloyd's finest film. It was certainly his most commercially successful, grossing $2.65 million (against production costs of just over $300,000), making *The Freshman* second only to Chaplin's *The Gold Rush* as the most financially successful film of the entire silent era.

The Phantom of the Opera (1925)

Directed by: Rupert Julian
Country: USA
Cast: Lon Chaney, Mary Philbin, Norman Kerry, Gibson Gowland

Perhaps Lon Chaney's most memorable film character was in the ground-breaking, frightening, Beauty-and-the-Beast-story *The Phantom of the*

Opera. Chaney plays Devil's Island escapee Erik – a vengeful and disfig-
ured composer who manifests himself as the ghost of the Paris Opera
(based on Gaston Leroux's 1911 novel). One of the film's great achievements was in its early use of two-colour Technicolor in the masked ball
sequence. The dark, expressionistic style of the rest of the film, undoubtedly drawing on some elements of *The Cabinet of Dr Caligari*, helped set

the tone for many of the classic Universal horror films of the 1930s. Often billed as 'The Man of a Thousand Faces', Chaney created his own make-up for every role, from hunchbacks to female disguises. The moment Christine (Philbin) unexpectedly tears off his concealing mask is still one of horror cinema's key images, and shocked audiences at the time. The skull-like, acid-scarred face, with darkened eye sockets, sharpened teeth and hollowed-out nostrils is an unforgettable sight. Photographs of the unmasked Phantom were banned from release before the film was seen, and this movie is one of the earliest to create the urban myth of 'fainting moviegoers'. The chandelier which falls during an opera performance may be more cinematically impressive, but it doesn't linger in the mind's eye in the way Chaney's scarred visage does.

Bronenosets 'Potyomkin'
Battleship Potemkin (1925)

Directed by: Sergei M. Eisenstein
Country: USSR
Cast: Alexander Antonov, Vladimir Barsky, Grigory Alexandrov

Hard to enjoy, perhaps, but easier to admire, *Battleship Potemkin* is a classic of Soviet revolutionary cinema, but its emphasis on the group over the individual doesn't connect as strongly with today's audiences. Split into five sections, the film is a fairly faithful (if dry) recounting of the failed 1905 Bolshevik revolution. The class distinctions between the sailors (enlisted men) and the officers (career military) are clearly represented through Eisenstein's 'montage' editing techniques. Best known is the oft-imitated 'Odessa Steps' sequence (a single page in the scenario, but the focus of the entire film) where Tsarist troops turn on the unarmed population. Eisenstein's use of close-ups and medium shots personalises the tragedy, engaging the viewers in the plight of individuals that make up the masses (the converse of the film's wider political concerns). Repeatedly cutting back to a baby in an unattended pram rolling down the steps, Eisenstein cranks up the tension. The lesson would be learned well by directors such as Alfred Hitchcock and Brian DePalma (*The Untouchables*, 1987).

Eisenstein originally set out to make a film about the 1904-05 war between Russia and Japan, but it was the cinematic potential of the Odessa Steps that saw him revise the project to focus on the Potemkin's sailors' uprising. *Battleship Potemkin* contained over 1,300 individual shots, at a time when the average Hollywood silent movie contained only around 700 and German films only 430 shots. The film was critically welcomed in London, Amsterdam, Moscow and Berlin upon release and was voted the best film ever made in 1948 and 1958. Douglas Fairbanks brought the film to America in 1926, where it was screened to great acclaim. It may be dated and didactic, but *Battleship Potemkin*'s symbolic editing influenced many later films.

The Gold Rush (1925)

Directed by: Charles Chaplin
Country: USA
Cast: Charlie Chaplin, Mack Swain, Tom Murray, Georgia Hale

Chaplin's little tramp goes gold prospecting in Alaska, blithely unaware he's being followed by a hungry grizzly bear. Sheltering in an isolated cabin, a wonderfully comic sequence sees him eat his boots due to hunger, and one of his companions hallucinates Chaplin as a chicken and proceeds to chase him into the snowy, cold wastes. The location later switches to the local gold rush town, where he pursues Georgia Hale. Chaplin often claimed that *The Gold Rush* was the film he wanted audiences and critics alike to remember him by. Many of the film's moments have since become identified with Chaplin rather than this particular film: the 'dance of the bread rolls', the 'chicken delusion', the 'boot eating' and the cabin that hangs off a cliff edge.

Inspired by tales of lost prospectors, Chaplin developed the story in 1923 and filming began in 1924, with his girlfriend, Lita Grey, as the female lead. Grey's pregnancy caused her to be replaced by Hale, resulting in much expensive re-shooting, which concluded in May 1925. Chaplin was still cutting the film between its two premieres on 26 June, in LA, and 16 August, in New York. *Vanity Fair* described *The Gold Rush* as 'Chaplin's greatest picture'.[14] The film cost $650,000 over 24 months and grossed $2.5 million in the US and a further $5 million internationally. Chaplin's personal profit from the film was $2 million. As he often did, Chaplin reissued a recut version of the film, with his own narration, in 1942. Whichever version is viewed, *The Gold Rush* is an undisputed classic and rated as one of the best films of the silent era.

Seven Chances (1925)

Directed by: Buster Keaton
Country: USA
Cast: Buster Keaton, T. Roy Barnes, Snitz Edwards, Ruth Dwyer

Keaton is Jimmy Shannon, set to inherit a family fortune, but only if he can find a bride before 7pm that same day. When he bungles a marriage proposal to his girlfriend, she unexpectedly turns him down. His other options (seven different women, his 'seven chances') spurn his advances. Finally, he takes the last resort of placing a newspaper advert calling for a prospective bride to meet him at a local church at 5pm. Unexpectedly, Keaton finds himself confronted by a veritable army of willing brides-to-be who pursue him into the hills. The film's end sees him trying to evade the attentions of 500 of them, all dressed in full wedding regalia, as he runs and trips down a steep hill, dodging hundreds of boulders of all sizes. The closing sequence was developed after preview audiences laughed when Keaton dislodged a couple of rocks as he rushed down the hill, and a re-shoot saw the joke extended to form the climax of a very funny film. Although it has been acclaimed as one of his best, Seven Chances was not a favourite of Buster Keaton himself, who didn't care for the movie until a New York Film Festival revival in 1965.

Based on a commercially unsuccessful play bought by his producer, Joe Schenck, the film came with director and screenwriter John McDermott attached; Keaton had no choice but to make it. Realising that McDermott planned a very faithful version of the failed play, Keaton quickly managed to replace him and re-worked the basic farce of the play into a much more layered comedy-drama. It was the material that Keaton changed and added to the play that made *Seven Chances* such a memorable film.

Faust (1926)

Directed by: FW Murnau
Country: Germany
Cast: Emil Jannings, Camilla Horn, Yvette Guilbert, Wilhelm Dieterle

Friedrich Wilhelm Murnau was one of the most important filmmakers of the cinema's first 35 years, yet his work is difficult to neatly categorise. Linked with the Weimar Germany group of directors, like Fritz Lang and G.W. Pabst, he finished his career in Hollywood. Following the horror film, *Nosferatu* (1922), he made a far less subtle work in his version of Goethe/Marlowe's *Faust*. Packed with memorable images and beautiful moments, like *The Thief of Bagdad*, the production values dominate. The Devil (Jannings) bets St Michael (Werner Futterer) he can tempt any human. With dominion over Earth as the prize, he attempts to turn alchemist Faust (Gosta Ekman) to evil. As the Devil spreads a disease through a small village, he simultaneously tempts Faust into a pact in return for the cure. The descent of the plague over the village as Mesiphtopheles throws the shadow of his cape across the community is one distinctive metaphorical scene among many, some of which undoubtedly appear heavy-handed today. Emil Jannings was suspended from wires for several hours to capture the shot of his cape billowing in the 'wind' (actually a series of electric fans blowing black soot onto a miniature village). The role of Gretchen (Horn) was initially offered to Lillian Gish (*Broken Blossoms*), but she declined when her preferred cameraman Charles Rosher was not hired. Actor Wilhelm Dieterle was also known as director William Dieterle who made *The Hunchback of Notre Dame* (1923) with Lon Chaney.

The General (1926)

Directed by: Buster Keaton and Clyde Bruckman
Country: USA
Cast: Buster Keaton, Marian Mack, Glen Cavender, Jim Farley

The General, a box office and critical failure upon initial release, was instrumental in the rehabilitation of Buster Keaton's reputation as a comic genius during the 1960s. Keaton plays a railroad engineer in the American South during the Civil War when, to impress his sweetheart, he tries to enlist in the Confederate Army. When spies steal his train and kidnap his girl, he's soon in comic pursuit. The story is loosely based upon a true incident, and Keaton went to great lengths to ensure the film's period authenticity. The story ranges from the epic to the personal, capturing the scope of the Civil War (often shown in the background of Keaton's comic business, featuring 500 members of the National Guard), while focusing on the increasingly farcical attempts of Keaton to retrieve his train and girl. A film of two halves, Keaton travels north on his stolen train before heading south again having rescued his girl. Many jokes and gags from the first half are repeated with a twist in the return journey. The climax sees Keaton bringing down a strategically important bridge, with the pursuing train on it. This gag was no model shot: it was done for real and the wreckage remained in the river in Oregon for many years. Despite the poor reviews and limited box office that greeted *The General*, it is perhaps the single most entertaining silent film of them all.

The Lodger: A Story of the London Fog (1926)

Directed by: Alfred Hitchcock
Country: UK
Cast: Ivor Novello, June Tripp, Marie Ault, Arthur Chesney

Made for Michael Balcon's new Gainsborough studios, *The Lodger* was Alfred Hitchcock's debut thriller, the film he recognised as the first true 'Hitchcock picture'. It was also his first critical and commercial success, even if his original intention to have Novello turn out to be the villain of the piece was thwarted by studio concerns. After a period working in Germany, Hitchcock had become well versed in the expressionist tradition evident in *The Cabinet of Dr Caligari* (1919) and *Nosferatu* (1922). The angular sets, stylised lighting and deep shadows were used to communicate the on-screen character's disturbed psychological states. It was a style that Hitchcock used effectively to mislead audiences into suspecting Novello's mysterious lodger of being a Jack the Ripper-style killer.

Written by Eliot Stannard and based on a best-selling novel by Hilaire Belloc's sister, Marie Belloc Lowndes, *The Lodger* established Hitchcock as a name director, but may also have trapped him into a career as a 'suspense' filmmaker. It could have been very different if the 'dreadful' film had been shelved as the distributor originally intended. Instead, Balcon fought for the film's release and had Hitchcock reshoot some rough-edged scenes. He also had the number of title cards significantly reduced, helping the flow. This reworked version was released in September 1926, only to be described in film trade journal *Bioscope* as '... possibly the finest British production ever made'.[15] There was another first in *The Lodger*: Hitchcock's cameo appearance as a newspaper editor, although the director insisted that his role only came about when the actor failed to show up. So are cinematic legends born.

Sunrise: A Song of Two Humans (1927)

Directed by: FW Murnau
Country: USA
Cast: George O'Brien, Janet Gaynor, Margaret Livingston, Bodil Rosing

Regarded by critics and film historians as one of cinemas most important films, *Sunrise* is FW Murnau's first American film and contains much that displays silent cinema as a unique art form distinct from post-1929 sound films. Whereas *Nosferatu* was a 'symphony', Murnau billed *Sunrise* as a 'song' and it is – at least in story terms – a far less complicated film. A simple country man, a farmer, is tempted into adultery by a sophisticated woman from the city; encouraged by her, he plots to murder his wife. Unable to carry through his intention, chance (or fate?) almost completes the job for him, and he returns to his marriage a better man.

There is much more to this dream-like film than a plot outline can convey. It is lush and lyrical, dramatic and impressive, a culmination of all the techniques of cinema developed across 30 years that made up the art of silent movies. The clash of city and country reflects a growing concern in the real-life of the 1920s as city life was growing to dominate. Represented in the film in terms of a visual poem, the country life is romanticised and idealised as much as the city and its inhabitants are demonised. Distinctive and never bettered, the film deservedly won a clutch of newly inaugurated awards called 'Oscars': it shared the first ever Best Picture Academy Award with *Wings* (1927), winning the Best Unique and Artistic Picture Award; Janet Gaynor received the first Best Actress Award; Karl

Struss and Charles Rosher shared the Best Cinematography Academy Award.

Metropolis (1927)

Directed by: Fritz Lang
Country: Germany
Cast: Gustav Froehlich, Brigitte Helm, Rudolph Klein-Rogge

A hundred years in the future, a high-tech city is maintained by a slave workforce for the benefit of a ruling elite, but revolution is brewing... Director Fritz Lang was clear that his ambition with *Metropolis* was to make the 'costliest and most ambitious picture ever'.[16] The idea came from his arrival (by ship) in the US in 1924 to promote the release of *Die Nibelungen* (1924) and the sight of the striking skyline of New York. A tour of the US studios further suggested that a film set in a gleaming city of the future would have to rival Hollywood films. The original intention (before Paramount's US editors savaged it) was to present a battle between science and the occult (some of the concept remains in the film as it exists today, but not as strongly as originally intended). Lang was determined to maintain a unity between his thematic concerns and the look of the film. His trademark montage editing (workers as cattle being literally 'fed' into the mouth of the great machine, for example) makes *Metropolis* a great work of agit-prop, as well as a fantastic warning of a machine-driven future for mankind. Meticulous miniature photography brought this modern city to life, while full-scale floods, explosions and riots greeted its inhabitants. Still impressive today is the sequence featuring the creation of the robot duplicate Maria, whose design influenced modern cinematic droids such as C-3PO in the *Star Wars* saga; and the city of Ridley Scott's *Blade Runner* could not have existed without *Metropolis*.

Napoléon (1927)

Directed by: Abel Gance
Country: France
Cast: Albert Dieudonné, Antonin Artaud, Pierre Batcheff, Gina Manès

French filmmaker Abel Gance's *Napoléon* was one of the most anticipated movies in the history of film. Shot on exotic locations, with a cast of thousands, and retelling a classic story of French history celebrating national heroism, the film premiered in April 1927 at the Paris Opéra to a full house and ran for three hours and forty minutes. Eliciting a 15-minute standing ovation from his audience, Gance used three side-by-side screens, making an enormous triptych, over forty feet wide. Gance filmed several pivotal scenes of his movie with three cameras, intending to create a widescreen vista. He called this technique 'Polyvision' and it clearly anticipated such 1950s cinematic gimmicks as Cinerama and VistaVision. Gance cleverly used his three-screen set-up to impress, having Napoleon ride his white horse, for example, across all three screens. By running different images on each screen, or a different image in the centre screen, Gance created what he called 'a new alphabet of cinema. I had only to create the grammar.'[17] Gance had set to out provide ever-greater realism in the cinema, to make the images giant and indistinguishable from reality. Instead, he had created a new form of abstraction, a way of displaying montage editing to create new meanings.

Un Chien Andalou/The Andalusian Dog (1928)

Directed by: Luis Buñuel and Salvador Dali
Country: France
Cast: Simonne Mareuil, Pierre Batchef, Luis Bunuel, Salvador Dali

Wilfully bizarre, *Un Chien Andalou* has been acclaimed as a surrealist masterpiece. Unlike mainstream silent movies of the time, in which storytelling was paramount, *Un Chien Andalou* deliberately dispenses with any easily accessible narrative flow. Luis Buñuel and Salvador Dalí created a series of disconnected scenes, and as a result came up with some of the most striking visuals in the entire history of cinema. The opening image alone sees a man (Buñuel himself) sharpening a cutthroat razor, which he then appears to use to slice a woman's eye (it was in fact a cow eye that was used to make the film). From images of nuns, through nudity and ants, grand pianos and dead donkeys, *Un Chien Andalou* confuses and confounds, yet remains engaging.

So, what are the themes? The eternals of life, death, lust and love are discernable, if viewers can decipher the juxtapositions of the bizarre images. In his autobiography, Buñuel sourced the film as having come from 'an encounter between two dreams'.[18] There's certainly a great deal of dreaming crammed into the film's 17 minutes, enough to have kept critics and academics debating its meaning for almost 80 years. The film allowed Buñuel to explore his 'passion for the irrational'[19] and to subvert reality as portrayed in cinema. His original intention was to add to the surreal nature of the film experience by burning the negative after it had completed distribution, thus destroying the work. Thankfully, that didn't happen and *Un Chien Andalou* can continue to confuse and infuriate to this day.

La Passion et la Mort de Jeanne d'Arc
The Passion of Joan of Arc (1928)

Directed by: Carl Theodor Dreyer
Country: France
Cast: Maria (Renée) Falconetti, Eugene Silvain, André Berley

Carl Dreyer's 1928 masterpiece is about the trial and death of France's fifteenth century warrior-saint, Joan of Arc. Denounced and nearly destroyed (just like the film's heroine), this movie faced the wrath of censors in France and the UK upon release. Dreyer's original negative was destroyed in a fire at the German studio UFA, but he managed to construct a new negative from alternate takes, which was then destroyed at another fire at the French studio where it was stored. Dreyer's excessive use of close-ups and bizarre shots – such as an upside-down-and-reversed shot of English soldiers, as well as a seemingly 'swinging' camera – appears to move the film into the realm of the avant-garde, although the director preferred the term 'emotional documentary'.[20] Dreyer's actors were denied make-up and he initially dropped the credits – echoing the earliest days of films when actors went uncredited – all to increase the audience's belief in the reality of the harrowing story of Joan's sacrifice. Despite this 'realism', the film is one of a series of stylised silent movies featuring the work of production designer Hermann Warm (*The Cabinet of Dr. Caligari*), who was inspired by medieval woodcuts and surrealism. The film cost an epic $9 million francs, which was spent on the impressive sets and a lengthy shoot. There are over 1,300 shots in the finished work, over twice the number found in an average feature film of the period. Above all, it is the dramatic and engaging performance of Falconetti as Joan, which has allowed Dreyer's *Passion* to stand the test of time.

Die Büchse der Pandora/Pandora's Box (1929)

Directed by: G.W. Pabst
Country: Germany
Cast: Louise Brooks, Fritz Kortner, Franz Lederer, Carl Goetz

Unusually for a Hollywood starlet, Louise Brooks, then 22-years-old, went to Germany to find fame in a series of iconic 1920s roles, beginning with *Pandora's Box*, a melodrama of lust and violence, which sees the central character of Lulu (Brooks) put through the ringer. She seduces a wealthy Count and his son, is convicted of the Count's murder and then escapes, only to fall victim to Jack the Ripper. Trained as a dancer, Brooks brings an ethereal touch to her otherwise naturalistic acting style; she is the centre around whom the melodrama revolves. The director of photography on this luminous movie was Gunther Krampf, who had filmed Murnau's *Nosferatu* in 1922. Brooks played a character poles apart from Lulu in the same year for Pabst in *Das Tagebuch einer Verlorenen/The Diary of a*

Lost Girl (1929): a single mother who eventually loses her child. However, *Pandora's Box* cemented Brook's screen persona and forever enshrined her in the annals of cinema history. Her iconic bobbed hairstyle, overt sexual confidence and defiant attitude was captured on celluloid and projected into the minds of millions. Her portraits became a precursor of those of James Dean and Marilyn Monroe: images of the kind of impossible beauty which only cinema can create.

City Lights (1931)

Directed by: Charles Chaplin
Country: USA
Cast: Charles Chaplin, Virginia Cherrill, Harry Myers, Henry Bergman

The last great silent film, *City Lights* was released two years after the coming of sound. Chaplin's little tramp is mistaken by a blind flower seller (Cherrill) as a millionaire (due to the sound of a nearby car). Saving a genuine drunken millionaire from a suicide attempt, Chaplin moves into his home, further cementing the blind girl's belief that he's rich. After many adventures, the millionaire gives Chaplin the money to pay for an operation to restore the girl's sight. The film's emotional climax sees the girl recognise her benefactor's true nature.

Chaplin began making *City Lights* in 1928, before sound cinema replaced silent film, and it took three years to complete. A six-month delay was caused when actor Henry Clive was fired from his role of the millionaire. Chaplin also fired Cherrill (for lateness), replaced her with *The Gold Rush*'s Georgia Hale, then re-hired her when Hale proved unsuitable. Chaplin's slow working methods, during which time he developed his intricate comedy business, meant that a technological revolution had taken place in Hollywood by the film's completion. While some could have been re-shot as a part-talkie, Chaplin decided that sound was 'not essential' to the success of his kind of cinema.

Chaplin avoided any significant use of sound until *The Great Dictator* (1940). However, he did lampoon talking films in *City Lights* by replacing

the speeches of civic dignitaries at the beginning of the film with kazoo noises. Despite it coming at the end of the silent era, *City Lights* was one of Chaplin's personal favourites: it combines the slapstick and humour of his best shorts with a level of emotional engagement rarely achieved in star-driven comedies.

THE COMING OF SOUND

The arrival of sound cinema was not only a technological development that would change the nature of film entertainment forever, it also signalled the end of the art of silent cinema. Movies had never been genuinely silent. From the earliest days, audiences vocally reacted to the moving wonders on screen, making cinema attendance a lively pastime. Many early films, especially those that toured the vaudeville circuit, came with musical accompaniment on a piano (or sometimes a full orchestra) and often a narrator, who would fill in narrative gaps or otherwise enhance the experience. Some 'event' movies would have specific scores composed for them, such as Saint-Saëns work for *L'Assassinat du Duc de Guise* (1908) or Shostakovich's score for *New Babylon* (1929). Live sound effects were also performed alongside the screening of a 'silent' film. The 'talkies', however, brought synchronised sound to film, and cinema as an art form changed forever. Colour, widescreen images and digital projection would follow and have had equally seismic effects on cinema.

French critic André Bazin saw such technological innovations (digital technology, of course, came after his time) as moving cinema ever closer to a more accurate representation of reality, an 'ultra realism'. Others, however, recognised the opposite: that each technological innovation somehow reduced the essential essence of 'cinema' that had been captured during the 30 years or so of the silent era. Each new innovation brought with it a series of representations, constructions and conventions that were no 'realer' in representing reality than the Lumière brothers pointing a primitive camera at a train entering a station.

From the earliest days of cinema there were experiments in synchronising sound with the newly captured images that were amazing audiences worldwide. Edison managed to connect a phonograph to his Kinetoscope and thus provide a soundtrack, and in 1913, Edison's company publicly screened films with sound using this system in New York. Gaumont in France had a similar system as early as 1901, while in 1909 in Britain Cecil Hepworth and James Williamson developed a system called Vivaphone. None of these systems progressed very far due to poor amplification (which meant the sound failed to travel enough distance in theatres) and the cumbersome, erratic nature of the devices.

Recording, reproduction and amplification systems developed by AT&T (American Telephone & Telegraph) provided the technological breakthrough necessary, at least in the presentation side of sound film exhibition. It was to be the growing corporations rather than the lone inventor who would develop such technology and the business model required for sound cinema. Progress resulting from World War I also fed into the development of sound-on-disc (AT&T/Bell Laboratories) and sound-on-film (General Electric) systems that emerged in the early 1920s.

Curiously, the newly emerging film 'moguls' who were running the studios at the end of the 1920s were not all that interested in sound. Adolph Zukor saw the coming of sound as disruptive to the established business of silent film production and distribution which, if it remained unchanged, had many years of commercial exploitation left in it. Paramount had invested strongly in new cinemas in the early 1920s and was extremely reluctant to now install sound systems. The studios would find themselves in the same situation at the start of the twenty-first century when, having invested in analogue multiplexes worldwide, the coming of digital creation and projection of movies threatened to derail a solidly established business model.

In the 1920s, rival technologies from different studios and corporations threatened to derail the whole process (just as the VHS vs Betamax video debate of the 1980s or Blu-Ray vs HD-DVD battle in the DVD era did). The biggest fear in Hollywood regarding the inevitable coming of sound was the loss of foreign, non-English speaking markets. Cinema stars like Charlie Chaplin and Mary Pickford were recognised the world over and their films exported to every country with a cinema exhibition circuit. With sound, the majority of the world's cinema market would be closed off to English-language Hollywood product.

In 1925, Western Electric demonstrated a sound-on-disc system that began to change attitudes to sound cinema in Hollywood. Warner Bros. President, Harry Warner, was taken with the new technology, believing it would give his studio an edge over the competition. His first thought was to synchronise music to the company's output of short films, which toured the vaudeville circuits of America. In the 1920s, Warner Bros. was the underdog of Hollywood studios, boasting John Barrymore and canine performer Rin-Tin-Tin as their top stars, and Ernst Lubitsch as the star director. Attracting Wall Street financing – a first for a movie studio – Warners bought Vitagraph, its distribution network and a chain of cinemas. In the future, such vertical integration would become illegal, but in the 1920s it was the ideal way for Harry Warner to challenge the other Hollywood studios. The development of sound cinema was to be next.

Developing the Vitaphone system, Warner Bros. released their first sound films on 6 August 1926. The programme included a speech from censor Will Hays welcoming sound, and the movie *Don Juan* (1926), starring John Barrymore and featuring a synchronised musical score (but no sound dialogue). A second Warner's Vitaphone programme followed in October that year to equally buoyant box office takings. Sound seemed to be the way forward for cinema, but the other studios were much more cautious than gung-ho Warner Bros. Possibly they had more to lose. A secret summit of the big five studios – Paramount, Universal, MGM, First National (later part of Warners) and Producers' Distributing Corporation – met in December 1926 and agreed that none of them would adopt sound until all of them did, and when they did they agreed they must all use the same, compatible system. In a seeming act of spite, they also decreed that whatever system was going to be adopted, it wouldn't be

Mitchell camera

Warners' preferred system. The innovator would, it seemed, be punished by the industry that would eventually benefit from the innovation.

Fox, run by William Fox, was not part of the 'big five' and, like Warner Bros., was a struggling studio. They purchased a sound-on-film system known as Movietone that premiered sound movies in a series of shorts in January 1927. April saw the arrival of the soon-to-be-famous Movietone newsreels with synchronised sound. Whereas Warner's Vitaphone system involved cumbersome sound discs, Movietone was flexible enough to be used on location, as in the recording of the launch of Charles Lindbergh's May 1927 first solo transatlantic flight to Paris.

In October 1927 Warner Bros. and Vitaphone broke new ground with the release of *The Jazz Singer* (1927), the now-famous 'first' sound movie that featured Al Jolson declaring, 'You ain't heard nothing yet!' *The Jazz Singer* actually only contained four segments with synchronised sound featuring some Jolson songs and that brief piece of dialogue. It was by no means a 'sound' film. However, the point had been made and the floodgates were opened. Many shorts featuring full dialogue were released and several films shot as silent movies were retooled for sound, such as Harold Lloyd's *Welcome Danger* (1929), Laurel and Hardy's cleverly titled *Unaccustomed As We Are...* (1929) and Alfred Hitchcock's *Blackmail* (1929).

By 1928, the big five studios had agreed to adopt a Western Electric-developed sound-on-film system (based on Movietone), consigning Warner Bros. breakthrough Vitaphone technology to the garbage heap of history. Transportation of the fragile Vitaphone discs would have undermined the Warner Bros. system eventually, and the studio discontinued it in 1930.

The first true all-dialogue feature film was a Vitaphone gangster film called *The Lights of New York* (1928), released in July 1928. That November, Paramount released its first talkie, *Interference* (1928). Within a year, 75 per cent of all Hollywood feature films would include a significant sound sequence or more. It took a while for the theatrical exhibition business to remodel the nation's cinemas for sound, so demand for silent films continued and many movies were released in sound and silent versions for a number of years until around 1931. This helped maintain Hollywood's hegemony abroad for a few more years, too.

Production of early sound films was difficult. The cameras were bulky and noisy, meaning that the recording systems would pick up the sound of the cameras operating and that they were largely immobile. The solution to the camera sound problem of encasing the camera in a soundproof booth served only to exacerbate the mobility problem. The limited range of the microphones meant actors had to congregate around hidden microphones (often in pot plants) to deliver their often-stilted dialogue. Many silent stars had voices unsuitable for sound, so their careers crashed-and-burned. Others, such as Laurel and Hardy took to sound easily and found, in fact, that it enhanced their art. Some, like Chaplin, were determined to stick with silent films, so extending his art. Much of the volatile atmosphere of the time is captured in the Gene Kelly movie musical *Singin' in the Rain* (1952). For many critics, the free-flowing art form of cinema had reverted to nothing more than filmed theatre.

Gradually, cinema techniques developed and adapted, as did the sound technology, so cameras were freed up and actors became more relaxed. Cinematic visions returned, but now with added sound, as in King Vidor's *Hallelujah!* (1929) and Lewis Milestone's *All Quiet on the Western Front* (1930). Innovative directors found ways of using sound that was unique to each of their films, such as the 'knife' dialogue in Britain's first sound film, Alfred Hitchcock's *Blackmail* (1929).

Inevitably, acting styles changed with the coming of dialogue. Silent stars had previously relied on gesture and facial expression, as well as dramatic exaggeration, to communicate emotions, moods and motivations. Now, such emotions were more easily expressed in words. Verbal and character-based comedy shot in studios replaced the freewheeling slapstick location-based chase comedy of the Keystone Kops and Mack Sennett. Although they lost out in the battle over sound technology, Warner Bros. found itself elevated to top studio status thanks to its breakthroughs in sound cinema and its development of the social realist gangster film through the 1930s. Fox, too, grew to become a major studio forming the basis of today's 20th Century Fox media empire.

In an attempt to extend their share of the market in foreign territories, where the conversion to sound cinema was slow, Hollywood studios began to make alternate language versions of their biggest films. Several Laurel and Hardy films exist in foreign language variations, with the stars learning their new dialogue phonetically and re-enacting scenes with largely foreign-language casts. Soon enough, national cinemas around the world would adapt to sound film and Hollywood would retreat to domination of the English-speaking cinema world, while continuing to export audio-dubbed product abroad.

By 1932, the conversion to sound cinema was virtually complete across the US. The rest of the world followed, with smaller companies with fewer cinemas converting more rapidly than larger countries with more mature film businesses and distribution systems. Eventually, those who didn't adapt quickly enough would go out of business. As the production of silent films was phased out, by the mid-1930s, sound came to dominate the medium of cinema, including international film production and exhibition. The age of silent cinema had come to an end.

SILENT CINEMA RESOURCES

DVD

As the availability of silent movies on DVD constantly changes (and improves) all the time, any list of particular titles is bound to date very quickly. Most of the films listed in Chapter 10 are available. Regular checks at Amazon or Play or other online DVD retailers will reveal the latest titles available. Checking www.silentera.com for new release information is highly recommended.

BOOKS

The following books on various aspects of the silent era were consulted in the writing of this book and come highly recommended.

Basinger, Jeanine, *Silent Stars*, Wesleyan University Press, 1999

Brownlow, Kevin, *The Parade's Gone By*, The University of California Press, 1992

Cousins, Mark, *The Story of Film*, Pavillion, 2004

Everson, William K., *American Silent Film*, Da Capo, 1998

Eyman, Scott, *The Speed of Sound: Hollywood and the Talkie Revolution 1926-1930*, The Johns Hopkins University Press, 1999

Ezra, Elizabeth, *French Film Directors: Georges Méliès*, Manchester University Press, 2000

Finler, Joel W., *Silent Cinema*, BT Batsford, 1997

Finler, Joel W., *The Hollywood Story*, Wallflower Press, 2003 (3rd ed)

Grieveson, Lee & Krämer, Peter (eds), *The Silent Cinema Reader*, Routledge, 2004

Izod, John, *Hollywood and the Box Office 1895-1986*, Macmillan Press, 1988

Louvish, Simon, *Keystone: The Life and Times of Mack Sennett*, Faber and Faber, 2003

Mitchell, Glenn, *The Chaplin Encyclopedia*, Batsford, 1997

Mitchell, Glenn, *The A-Z of Silent Comedy*, Batsford, 1999

Monaco, James, *How to Read a Film*, Oxford University Press, 1981

Robinson, David, *Chaplin: His Life and Art*, William Collins & Sons, 1985

Thomson, David, *A Biographical Dictionary of Film*, Andre Deutsch, 1994

Thompson, Kristin & Bordwell, David (eds), *Film History: An Introduction*, McGraw-Hill Inc, 1994

Wyver, John, *The Moving Image*, Blackwell/BFI, 1989

WEBSITES

General

www.silentera.com

One of the finest silent cinema websites featuring news of new discoveries and new DVD releases and a host of resources relating to the history of silent cinema. Includes a constantly changing Top 100 Silent Era Films list, voted on by readers/users. Indispensable.

www.silentsaregolden.com/

Photo-led silent movies fan site. Also includes contemporary material and silent era essays.

www.welcometosilentmovies.com

Up-to-date and active silent movies site covering events and new releases, as well as silent movie history.

www.nwlink.com/~erick/silentera/Silent.html

Mini biographies of silent era personalities, behind and in front of the cam-era. Includes William S. Hart, George Méliès, Fritz Lang and Paul Wegener.

www.screenonline.org.uk/education/student/auteur/tour2.html

A British Film Institute website dealing with the British silent movie business.

www.tc.umn.edu/~yahnk001/film/cinema1.htm

A potted history of silent movies.

www.reel.com/reel.asp?node=features/millennium/silent

Five defining films from the silent era: *Birth of a Nation*, *Sherlock Jr*, *Battleship Potemkin*, *The Big Parade*, *Metropolis*.

www.cinemaweb.com/silentfilm/bookshelf/

Original newspaper features and film reviews collected from the silent era.

www.seeing-stars.com/Theatres/SilentMovie.shtml

The website for Hollywood's rightly-celebrated Silent Movie Theatre.

Silent Stars

www.busterkeaton.com

Official Buster Keaton website.

www.charliechaplin.com

Official Charlie Chaplin website.

www.haroldlloyd.com

Official Harold Lloyd website.

www.marypickford.com

Home site of the Mary Pickford Institute.

http://douglasfairbanks.org/

The Douglas Fairbanks online museum.

http://silent-movies.org/Arbucklemania//home.html

Roscoe Arbuckle fan website.

http://slapstick-comedy.com/Mabel/home.html

Mabel Normand fan website.

http://silent-movies.org/Taylorology/

An extensive, not to say obsessive, website delving into the minutiae of the William Desmond Taylor murder case.

NOTES

1   Toulet, E (1995) *Cinema is 100 Years Old*, trans S. Emmanuel, London, Thames and Hudson Ltd. Page 15.

2   Méliès, Georges (1912) 'Le Merveilleux au cinéma', *L'Echo de cinéma*, 24 mai. Pages 1-2. T

3   Premiere staff writers, 'The 50 Greatest Movie Stars of All Time', *Premiere*, April 2005, Vol.18, #7

4   Adolph Zuker, President of Paramount Pictures: "I started out giving her $500 per week, but I finally paid her $10,000." Quoted in: Basinger, Jeanine (1999), 'Mary Pickford', *Silent Stars*, Hanover and London, Wesleyan University Press/University Press of New England. Page 18.

5   Basinger, Jeanine (1999), 'Mary Pickford', *Silent Stars*, Hanover and London, Wesleyan University Press/University Press of New England. Page 52.

6   Quoted in: Thomson, David (1994, revised edition), 'Rudolph Valentino', *A Biographical Dictionary of Film*, London, Andre Deutsch. Page 766.

7   Thomson, David (1994, revised edition), 'Rudolph Valentino', *A Biographical Dictionary of Film*, London, Andre Deutsch. Page 766.

8   Mitchell, Glenn (1997), 'The Chaplin Craze', *The Chaplin Encyclopedia*, London, BT Batsford. Page 45.

9   Mitchell, Glenn (1997), 'The Chaplin Craze', *The Chaplin Encyclopedia*, London, BT Batsford. Page 45.

10 Thomson, David (1994, revised edition), 'Buster Keaton', *A Biographical Dictionary of Film*, London, Andre Deutsch. Page 390.

11 Fairbairn, Forbes W. (1920), No headline, *The Los Angeles Examiner*, Los Angeles, Hearst, September 13, 1920. Online at: http://www.public.asu.edu/~ialong/Taylor33.txt

12 Cousins, Mark (2004), 'The World Expansion of Style (1918-28)', *The Story of Film*, London, Pavillion. Page 103.

13 Kendrick, John (2003), 'A witches' brew of fact, fiction and spectacle', *Kinoeye* Vol.3, #11, October 13, 2003. Online at: http://www.kinoeye.org/03/11/kendrick11.php

14 Mitchell, Glenn (1997), 'The Gold Rush', *The Chaplin Encyclopedia*, London, BT Batsford. Page 113.

15 *Bioscope*, September 16 1926. Online at: http://www.screenonline.org.uk/film/id/438120/index.html

16 Brandao, Rodrigo (2002), 'The Making of Metropolis', *Metropolis Press Book*, New York, Kino International. Page 14.

17 Brownlow, Kevin (1983), *Napoleon: Abel Gance's Classic Film*, New York, Alfred A. Knopf.

18 Buñuel, Luis (1983), *My Last Breath*, London, Jonathan Cape.

19 Buñuel, Luis (1983), *My Last Breath*, London, Jonathan Cape.

20 Morris, Gary (2000), '*The Passion of Joan of Arc* on DVD', *Bright Lights Film Journal*, Issue#27, January 2000. Online at: http://www.brightlightsfilm.com/27/joanofarc.html

INDEX

kamera
BOOKS

ESSENTIAL READING FOR ANYONE INTERESTED
IN FILM AND POPULAR CULTURE

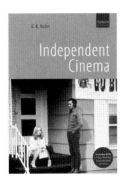

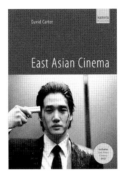

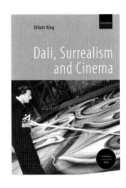

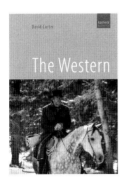

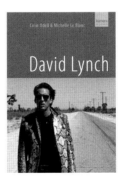

Tackling a wide range of subjects from prominent directors, popular
genres and current trends through to cult films, national cinemas
and film concepts and theories. Kamera Books come complete with
complementary DVDs packed with additional material, including feature
films, shorts, documentaries and interviews.

www.kamera.co.uk/kamerabooks

creative ESSENTIALS

OFFERING EASY-TO-FOLLOW ADVICE AND PRACTICAL
SOLUTIONS ON ALL ASPECTS OF FILMMAKING
AND MEDIA PRODUCTION

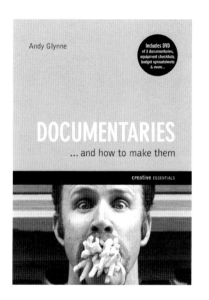

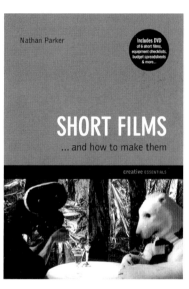

Creative Essentials provide accessible, comprehensive and affordable
how-to guides to a range of subjects, written by experts in their field.
They include case studies and in-depth analysis, practical advice,
interviews with key creatives and comprehensive resources guides
to funding bodies, distribution outlets, available courses, and come
complete with DVDs packed with additional material ranging from
shorts and extracts, to templates, spreadsheets, sample contracts,
release forms, checklists and more.

www.kamera.co.uk/creativeessentials

Sunrise Silent's *Silent Cinema Stars*

Extracts featured

01. Johnny Hines (*Conductor 1492*)
02. Mary Pickford (*Little Annie Rooney*)
03. Harold Lloyd (*I'm On My Way*)
04. Pola Negri (*Hotel Imperial*)
05. Rudolph Valentino (*Son of the Sheik*)
06. The Gish Sisters (*Orphans of the Storm*)
07. Douglas Fairbanks (*Wild & Woolly*)
08. Greta Garbo (*The Joyless Street*)
09. Laura La Plante (*Cat and the Canary*)
10. Buster Keaton (*Cops*)
11. Norma Talmadge (*The Social Secretary*)
12. Rin Tin Tin (*The Night Cry*)
13. Raymond Griffith (*The Night Club*)
14. Colleen Moore (*A Roman Scandal*)
15. Lon Chaney (*Phantom of the Opera*)
16. Louise Brooks (*It's the Old Army Game*)
17. Charles Chaplin (*The Star Border*)
18. Clara Bow (*My Lady of Whims*)
19. William S. Hart (*The Ruse*)
20. Pearl White (*The Perils of Pauline*)
21. Lige Conley (*Air Pockets*)
22. John Barrymore (*The Beloved Rogue*)
23. Theda Bara (*The Unchastened Woman*)
24. Our Gang (*The Big Show*)
25. Mabel Normand (*The Extra Girl*)
26. Alla Nazimova (*Salome*)
27. Gloria Swanson (*Teddy at the Throttle*)

Total running time: 193 minutes

WWW.SUNRISESILENTS.COM